The Sweet Sixteen

A Coach's Guide to Leadership

AUSTIN MCBETH

ISBN 978-1-0980-2530-4 (paperback)
ISBN 978-1-0980-2531-1 (digital)

Christian Faith Publishing, Inc.
832 Park Avenue
Meadville, PA 16335
www.christianfaithpublishing.com

Printed in the United States of America

Introduction

"Guys, I wouldn't trade you for another team in the country," he said emphatically, as if he were trying to stir up deep emotions of passion and desire in me to run through a wall for him. But those words fell straight to the floor before ever having the chance to make it the twelve inches from my head to my heart, as I'm sure he hoped it would. As I looked around the locker room at my teammates, I could feel their responses were the same as mine.

I wasn't naive enough to believe that there weren't at least a dozen teams that were clearly more talented than us and that coach wouldn't jump at the chance to make his own. It couldn't be true, especially after all the horrible things he'd said to me—the constant reminders of every one of my deficiencies and the fear-based system that he'd entrapped me in to get me to perform at the highest level. In some regard, the idea of riding the bench and being a cheerleader for my teammates seemed like a much more enjoyable role than my current one, having one eye on my defender and one on the man holding my leash on the sidelines. There were fewer things more demoralizing than playing in constant fear of the monster prowling the sidelines, always quick to chew someone out and then motion to the bench for someone to sub in for the accused. From my vantage point, I felt like the prime candidate to throw away and upgrade for a new and improved model. People would ask me, "Is it scary playing in front of a sold-out arena?" They were unaware that it wasn't the thousands of screaming fans that made my stomach do flips—it was the man dressed in a suit and tie that never seemed to be satisfied with my performance.

"Guys, the reason I yell and scream and push you is because I know how good you can be, and I have to get that out of you. But know this, I love you!" As if the beginning of the sentence wasn't hypocritical enough, those last three words tasted as bitter as a dark black roast coffee. You love me? Is this what love looks like from the closest thing I have to a father figure? Screaming words across the gym that I can't even get myself to retype, words that express what my Father in heaven describes Himself as *love*? Coach's face was as red as the bloodstain on my white tights, a result of diving on the floor for a loose ball, drops of spit accumulating in the corners of his mouth, taking flight toward my paralyzed body, and abusive screams startling everyone in the arena. Love is what motivates a coach to do that to a nineteen-year-old college sophomore for thinking his teammate was open on a backdoor cut but ended up turning the ball over by being a bit too ambitious.

The way I felt in those moments didn't feel right. There was a disconnect in my soul between when he would say he loves us and the gut-wrenching embarrassment that I felt as I was publicly dehumanized. Did coach actually love me, or was he merely trying to make me feel a sense of allegiance to the team by using such strong words? Would you, as a parent, be okay with a coach treating your son or daughter this way, when there was an expectation they would take care of your child? Or even worse, is it possible that some coaches don't know what love actually means?

This story is not my own, but it is the experience of many athletes that I'm afraid resonates with far too many damaged young men and women. It paints a picture of real situations I have dealt with firsthand, have been witness to, and have heard about from others. It is my desire in this book to expose these things and bring them to light for the purpose of the change that needs to happen in coaches at every level. My intention is not to put anyone who I have played for or coached with on blast, but I think this is a macrolevel problem that has gone unaddressed for far too long.

The more I am around the game of basketball and college athletics in general, the more I notice the egregious misuse of this powerful word on a daily basis. Program after program, loss after loss, and across multiple sports, I hear and see the contradiction of this sacred word and the actions following it.

The abuse of this word isn't just taking place emotionally and verbally either. The most gut-wrenching reality is that sexual abuse is running rampant in sports today. Coaches across the country have taken advantage of their position of authority to quench a lustful passion that instead of being overcome with self-control is stealing the innocence of countless boys and girls.

In 2011, Jerry Sandusky, a football coach at Penn State University, was indicted for fifty-two counts of child molestation. They believe that Coach Sandusky could have been taking advantage of athletes for as long as thirty plus years. Over the years, there were witnesses who came forward about the abuse, and staff members in the athletic department chose to disregard the victims' claims.

In September of 2016, USA Olympic Gymnastics team doctor Larry Nassar, gym owners, coaches, and other staff members were implicated for the sexual abuse of over 368 female athletes over the course of two decades. Larry Nassar was also charged on multiple counts of child pornography. Nassar, who was employed at Michigan State as a team doctor, also had witnesses come forward about the assaults, and they were covered up.

In October of 2018, AAU coach Greg Stephens was arrested and charged for posing as a girl on social media, in attempts to trick high school basketball players to send him naked pictures and videos. The charges also included Stephens secretly recording players taking showers during tournament trips and recording himself fondling players while they slept. They believe Stephens was involved with over four hundred players, primarily minors, before being charged.

This is unfortunately just the tip of the iceberg. According to Sylvie Parent, PhD, assistant professor, Department of Physical Education, and Karim El Hlimi, PhD student, Department of Physical Education, "The studies we currently have at our disposal show that between 2% and 8% of athletes (both minors and young adults) are victims of sexual assault within the context of sport. Based on certain hypotheses put forward in the past, it was said that elite young athletes were more likely to be sexually assaulted than their lower-level counterparts. This claim has since been confirmed by further research."

Is it just me, or is this a macrolevel problem that needs to stop? Is it "not a big deal" because "that's just what coaches do and say these days"? Or is it a lethal issue that is destroying more than just the countenance of a distressed point guard, who didn't want to disappoint his head coach, let alone lose the game?

Chapter 1

What Is Love?

I grew up in church. My single mother of two extremely rambunctious and obnoxious boys is the most dedicated and committed woman I know. I cannot recall a Sunday morning or Wednesday night that we weren't making the eighteen-minute drive from Wayland, Iowa, to Mount Pleasant for church at Faith Christian Outreach Church. Without the help of a father in the house, my mom saw to it that Proverbs 22:6 would be her goal, "Train up a child in the way he should go, and when he is old he will not depart from it." This was her standard for doing the impossible—being a single mother of two out-of-control boys.

So church is where you could find us—on the drama team and the praise and worship band, at summer youth camp, and every other area in which we could be involved. And we loved it! God was a very real and huge part of our lives, both individually and as a family. Because of my mom's dedication to church, the word love was no stranger to my vocabulary. I was just like every other teenage kid that flippantly used the word love to describe my affections toward things like basketball and the TV show *Boy Meets World*. But I also knew the word love in the context of God's Word. I knew verses such as John 3:16, "For God so loved the world that He gave His only begotten Son. That whosoever believes in him will not perish, but have everlasting life," and Proverbs 17:17, "A friend loves at all times." So when I hear "love" used incorrectly by coaches, it sounds the alarm in my heart, because of the truth I know about this word.

The word love is overused due to the English language only having one word for it. According to Merriam-Webster, a few definitions are as follows: (1) strong affection for another arising out of kinship or personal ties; (2) the object of attachment, devotion, or admiration; and (3) affection based on admiration, benevolence, or common interests. Because I have spent the majority of my life in church, I have learned that our English language has done a poor job of translating the word love in its entirety. We use the word love to describe everything—"I love pizza," "I love Christmas," "I love my wife," and "I love Sunday afternoon naps." These are all things that are commonly said today. We don't ascribe the same worth to all those things, yet we use the same word for all of them.

In Greek (the language in which the New Testament was originally written), there are four main words that we now blanket with the word "love":

- *Philià*—a brotherly/friendship love, which is where we get the name of the city Philadelphia
- *Èros*—a sexual/passionate love, which is where we get the term erotic
- *Storge*—the word to describe love for family or relatives

There are three more words to describe love, but the one I'm going to spend time on is the highest form of love, *agape*. Agape is defined as "divine love characterized by sacrifice in the pursuit of another person's good" (*Desiring God*). It is an unconditional love that transcends faults done by the receiver and always desires the best for them independent of what they can do for the giver.

Agape is the love that we, as human beings, desire from our closest companions, whether we know it or not. It is the security of knowing that our actions, mistakes, and shortcomings will never destroy the relationship. It is seeing a newborn baby laid on its mother's breast for the first time. It is seeing a video of a little girl collapse to the floor in tears as a man in uniform walks into her classroom right after returning to US soil, this overwhelming joy that brings viewers to uncontrollable tears. This is agape.

Daddy Issues

I didn't have a dad growing up. I have no memories of sitting in his lap while he was in "his chair" on a Sunday afternoon to watch the game. When friends would tell me stories of their camping adventure over the weekend with their dad, my reality was going to the gym to get shots up while my mom rebounded. I never experienced hearing the deep sound of my father's voice summoning me to the kitchen to sternly instruct me to "do as your mother told you to do." I did, however, have several amazing men in my life who, without knowing it, gave me glimpses of what it meant to be a good father. I also had a mother who to this day I honor more than anyone I have ever known, but there was still a longing for something that I not only wanted but also needed.

The sad truth is that the word divorce no longer creeps out of someone's mouth, as if it were as serious as the word cancer, like it used to. Growing up, people used to approach the topic of divorce with such hesitation, because of the weight it carried, but in 2019, it can be as casual to talk about as the six o'clock news. While parents separating from the covenant they committed to is becoming increasingly more of the social norm, the impact inside the home is still just as devastating.

Growing up, I was under the impression that my situation was normal. Sure, other people had two parents, but my life seemed to be just fine. We had an unwritten "don't ask, don't tell" rule when it came to the topic of my "never before seen" father, so I didn't know anything about him and didn't think about him too often. It wasn't until my late teenage years that I started to discover the emotional and mental barbed-wire fences that I started to run into. Not only did they keep me from experiencing the freedom that parental security brings, but also it hurt when I ran into new questions as to *why* he wasn't around.

According to the 2017 US Census Bureau data, representing children living without a biological, step, or adoptive father, over twenty-five percent of children in America are growing up without their biological father in the home—that's roughly 19.7 million children. We have millions of young men and women entering into adulthood having never learned the things that God designed the family (and more specifically a father) to teach them.

Whether it's popular in today's culture or not, God designed the family for a very important purpose. One father, one mother, and their children were orchestrated by the Creator of the universe to function like a well-balanced team—each individual designed to play a specific role in the household to glorify and point people back to Himself. However, because we have an enemy, who hates everything that God called good, he is out to destroy anything that brings glory back to the Father. This is why I firmly believe that issues of infidelity, children dishonoring parents, homosexuality, premarital sex, and parents being reprimanded for disciplining their children are so prevalent in our culture. Each and every one of those issues have slowly poisoned marriage or defiled God's intent for families.

Because of this tragic depletion of a God-designed family structure, young men and women are in constant search of certain emotional needs and direction that they aren't able to acquire anywhere else. Needs such as acceptance, approval, encouragement, comfort, security, affection, support, respect, attention, and appreciation are designed to be cultivated inside of every home. Then, after the children become adults and leave the house, they are supposed to transfer all those needs from their parents into God's hands to sustain, one day to find a spouse to start their own family with, and repeat the process with their own children. Unfortunately, Satan found a way to ruin that cycle—break up the home and leave the children emotionally deficient. My mother, as I said before, did a fantastic job raising Cameron and me. She did everything she could to make sure all of our needs were met; nevertheless she was never designed to be the sole provider of all those needs; they were meant to be shared between a mother and father.

Shedding light on dysfunction in families sets a magnifying glass on how a terribly large percentage of young adults come into their college experience deficient. Coaches need to understand that they are inheriting young men and women that may need as much grace in these areas as they need work on their jump shot. And whether coaches want this responsibility or not, they now play a huge role in the furthering of their players' emotional, mental, and spiritual growth. The gut-wrenching reality of my job as a collegiate basketball coach is that the statistics for African-American boys who grew up fatherless is significantly higher than the average, and they make up a majority of collegiate basketball players.

When any emotional need or deficiency resides inside of a person, there will always be fruit that is produced from what has been planted inside of the person. Too many times, we see bad behavior and want to fix the behavior without taking any thought as to the seeds that were planted in the person during their childhood that produced the fruit that we don't like.

For example, when a coach has a freshman that comes in and constantly argues with the staff and never thinks he's wrong, the typical response of a coach is to put him on the line and run him, to shout at him and make sure he knows who's in charge, and to tell him he will never step foot on the court until he realizes it's "my way or the highway." While I don't think the issue of disrespect should go unaddressed, I think it's important as a coach to put more value on the relationship and try to learn what deficiencies may have caused this type of disrespect.

When a player is doing a great job on the court, but is making poor decisions with what they're posting on social media, it seems simple to suspend them or ban them from social media. This attempt at behavior modification might stop the problem in the short term, but what about the root of why they think the behavior is acceptable? When the suspensions are no longer a threat to them, why would they have the wisdom to not continue the behavior? Do we truly care about the future maturity of our athletes, or do we care more about keeping them out of trouble so they can help us win games?

I want to challenge coaches to invest in the relationship, more than dwelling on the fruit that you don't like. The greatest part about approaching your players with this mind-set is when a player truly feels that you care about them and their well-being, they are so much more receptive to your standards. When they show up to practice late and you punish them for it, they are more receptive to your rebuke because of the relationship that is already established.

I am making a charge to every coach, mentor, and father who is brave enough to continue reading to take the challenge of being a living example of what God desires for you to do with your sphere of influence. It's easy to yell. It feels good to cuss out a player or your son when they've fallen short or made a mistake to "blow off some steam." It is difficult to have the self-control to hold your tongue and live a life that is consistent and excellent.

Coaches work tirelessly to be successful. It's the goal of every coach to cut down the nets at the end of their season. For me, I have always dreamt of celebrating with my team, as we attempt to leave our mark on the most coveted tournament of all time—March Madness. I still remember being seconds away, not once, but twice, from the Sweet Sixteen as a player at Iowa State. However, *The Sweet Sixteen* that this book is about will last much longer than a basketball game. It will fulfill you more than any victory. It comes only from the Word of God, and it will leave a legacy long after you're gone.

Chapter 2

Perfect Love

*There is no fear in love. But perfect love drives out fear,
because fear has to do with punishment. The one
who fears is not made perfect in love.*

—1 John 4:18

1 John 4:18 makes a strong declaration that love and fear cannot coexist. It then goes on to give its reasoning—fear and punishment have a strong correlation. At the very root of fear is the presence of the potential for a negative consequence. Children are afraid of the dark because of what could potentially harm them that they cannot see. A master's student is afraid of taking her final exam because of the lurking plausibility of her future being compromised if she fails. Both fears are motivated by the same thing—there is an outcome on the other side of this that could hurt.

I find it remarkable that of all the things God could have said love is not, He chose fear. But I am very grateful that He did, because I believe it helps illuminate how we, as God's creation and workmanship, have overlooked this truth. The existence of fear-based motivation disguised as love is everywhere. It is in our homes, our schools, and our marriages and it is corrupting our sports.

On a daily basis, we as coaches say things like, "If one more person misses a layup, we'll just stop practicing and run for the next hour." "If you guys don't pick up the energy, I'm gonna sub every last one of you out and you won't play the rest of the game." "If I find out any of you are at a party this weekend, we'll practice at five o'clock Monday morning." The examples go on and on.

Now, some of you might think there's nothing wrong with giving consequences to your team, and I agree with you. However, it's all about the message that is being sent to your players. Do they understand that consequences are part of the decisions and choices that we make in life? Or do they constantly live scared that if they aren't perfect, then they will be punished? One perspective is healthy, that they are accountable for their actions, and it takes a lot of work to be successful. The other leaves them constantly worried of never living up to a coach's expectations and will always fall short.

The introduction of this book expressed my heart's inability to understand how a coach could treat players with such disrespect and anger and still claim to love them. I believe that the Word of God is clear that a coach cannot operate in a fear-based coaching style and also claim to love them. They must either stop telling the player something that simply isn't true or begin to change the way they treat and motivate their players.

I believe there is a misconception that if a coach doesn't yell, swear, and punish their team for every mistake, then they will be looked at as soft and the team will not perform to its full potential. This is a lie that coaches have believed that has been reinforced by demonstrative coaches having successful teams. People have equated success to being angry and yelling to get the most out of their players. I'm a firm believer that a coach can have standards, and high standards at that, and have a team that meets those expectations without being a tyrant. After all, people are able to accomplish so much more when they are motivated by the power of love, not fear.

In many situations, the truth is that coaches are prideful and don't handle failure well. It's not the true motivation of the coach to degrade their players for the betterment of their overall performance. At the root of the issue, it's the coach dealing with their own personal struggles by lashing out to burn off steam. The scary part about this problem is that it can easily be twisted to come across like something it's not in attempt for the coach to save face. I would like to encourage any coach that struggles with this, and is feeling convicted right now, that you can change. If you are a believer and have a relationship with Jesus Christ, through the power of the Holy Spirit, you can begin to exhibit the fruit of the spirit that is self-control. And what better way to proclaim the power of the gospel than to be transformed from someone who used to struggle with controlling their temper to someone that was changed by the power of God!

Whether it's a belief that scaring players into playing better or needing to lash out to deal with deep-rooted pride is something that describes you, I pray the following truth of God's Word will begin to heal your heart and transform your mind.

*****

When we think of love, it's very common to think of a picturesque image of two people sitting on the hood of a car watching the sun set, wrapped up under a blanket while enjoying the stillness of the evening. Hollywood has done a great job of making love appear to be an explosion of chemicals in the brain that takes a person to a euphoric dimension, unable to be accurately described with words, a feeling that spurs a human to do things they would never do under different circumstances. The problem is Hollywood did not create love. Humans did not create love. God created it, because He *is* love. It's not a gift that He delivers to the worthy and the unworthy, as if it were a token of His appreciation. It is the essence of His being.

Because Genesis 1:26–28 says that we were created in the image and likeness of God, we were designed with the capacity to replicate who He is. This is why directly following the explanation that fear and love cannot coincide, verse 19 says, "We love because he first loved us." When we experience this *agape*, we experience the nature of the God who created us in His image.

When the truth of *agape* is revealed, it sheds a glorious light into the darkness of how we flippantly misuse its name and misappropriate it with something as trivial and fleeting as feelings. So if love is not a feeling and God has given us the ability to love, by first expressing it to us and embedding it in our DNA, then how do we know what it looks like?

> Love is patient, love is kind. It does not envy, it does not boast, it is not proud. It does not dishonor others, it is not self-seeking, it is not easily angered, it keeps no record of wrongs. Love does not delight in evil but rejoices with the truth. It always protects, always trusts, always hopes, always perseveres. Love never fails. (1 Corinthians 13:4–8a)

This is love. If you have ever had questions about the character of God as to what He is truly like, these sixteen traits should give you understanding. Not only does this provide a window into the nature of God, but also it provides a mirror in which we can judge our reflection. What I find fascinating about the description of love is that you will not find any feelings at all, not one. Love, in its totality, is entirely made up of choices. They are all action verbs. So if love doesn't have anything to do with feelings and is solely based on choices, then everyone is capable of loving anyone, correct?

Does this not make more sense than the counterargument? As I talked about earlier, John 3:16 says that God so loved the *world*! There is good reason to believe that not everyone in the world is deserving of love from the Almighty God. However, this *agape* that describes our perfect Savior isn't hindered by whether we are deserving. It is a choice made by the Giver. This is the good news of the gospel! When I was undeserving of God *feeling* like loving me, He made the *choice* to send His Son to the cross anyway! I believe that for some of you reading this, the truth of God's love alone is able to set you free from doubt, fear, and shame. Be encouraged today. God chose to send His only begotten Son to die for you before you even had the chance to love Him back. And because God knows the end from the beginning (Isaiah 46:10), He knew that multitudes of people would refuse to love Him back and still sentenced His only Son to death for those people anyway. I am forever humbled when I go to use the word love, because of this example of perfect love.

Earlier, I talked about how *agape* was an unconditional love that transcends faults done by the receiver and always desires the best for them, independent of what they can do for the giver. That answers the question of *how* we are called to love. These characteristics in 1 Corinthians 13 answers for us *what* it practically looks like. Please hear me when I say this is a full-time job. I would go as far as to say that it is impossible for anyone who tries to accomplish this under their own strength. But praise be unto God that He gives us the Holy Spirit to strengthen us to accomplish what we cannot on our own.

What implications does this have on our lives moving forward? It gives us our standard of conduct mapped out in a blueprint for our relationships. If we are truly committed to loving our players the way God calls us to, it starts and ends with these attributes. When you look intently at what love looks like, you will quickly realize that the stereotypical coach struggles in the majority of these areas.

As parents, I think it is imperative that you encourage your children to spend time during their recruiting process to do some vetting of their own. It is very easy, as a coach, to sit down with a recruit and paint a picture that is appealing, to say all the right things, and to come across as a "player's coach" to whom anyone would want to give their allegiance to. The problem is talk is cheap. A coach's true colors might be able to be suppressed during a meeting or a practice when a recruit and their parents are sitting courtside watching their every move, but in the heat of competition, the real coach surfaces.

When I was a senior in high school, I was being recruited by two junior colleges, and they happened to be playing each other at a nearby location, so my mom and I went to watch the game. As the action was in full swing, I was locked in on the size of the players, the pace of play, and new moves I could put in my arsenal. Meanwhile, my incredibly insightful mother was focused on something entirely different. She leaned over and disrupted my laser focus to draw my attention to the bench of the home team. "I want you to watch how that coach is acting," she said with a tone that I quickly recognized was a very serious one. As play went on, I noticed how every little thing sent the coach into a rage. He was stomping his size 15 shoe into the court each time he was displeased or grabbing a guy by the jersey on the bench and shoving him toward the scorer's table, when he wanted him to check in. There was so much anger in his eyes as he paced back and forth down the sideline. "If that's how he treats his players in public, Austin, imagine what he's like behind closed doors in practice."

That day changed my life. At the time, I thought it merely deterred me from wanting to commit to that school. As a senior in high school, I didn't think I would be coaching, so the impact of that day didn't surface until years later. I truly believe it is so important as a recruit and a parent to experience a head coach in person during a game to assess his character. Sitting in an office decorated with trophies, accolades, and high-quality pictures from past games is where you meet the representative of a coach. It's calculated, planned out, and typically a coach putting their best foot forward. I'm not saying all coaches lie to players when they meet with them, but what I am saying is you don't get the full scope of who they are.

Do yourself a favor and treat the recruiting process the same as coaches do. When a coach is interested in a player, they typically make that decision off a highlight tape or watching them live in one game. After they decide that the player is talented enough to play for them, that's when the real work begins. They want to see their transcript and know what their GPA is. They want to talk to their parents and find out about their family situation and homelife. They will usually speak to their AAU and high school coach so they can get two different vantage points on their character, work ethic, coachability, and IQ. The process is very detailed and very intentional. Why would a young man or young lady not do the same when deciding who they're going to hand over the next four years of their life to?

*****

Because of the rise in sports and the demands that are put on winning, what God deems as love is slowly being uprooted and replaced with the chase for the "Almighty W." I will be the first to admit that college athletics has turned into somewhat of an all-consuming fire that has radically impacted our country. Just into basketball alone, the amount of money spent across the country on third-grade AAU alone would probably make a significant dent in our country's debt. The chance to get a college scholarship and eventually one day make it to the NBA is now one out of every ten kid's goal (another thirty percent of those kids are focused on the MLB, the NFL, and the PGA tour). Playing sports at a young age is becoming less about enjoying the game and having fun and more about "setting ourselves up to get a scholarship."

I don't think we should stifle any young person's desire to get a college scholarship and be excellent at their gift, but I think it has polluted the sports world at every level into being only concerned with winning. Please don't misunderstand me—I love to win. I actually think I hate losing more than I enjoying winning, but the fact remains the same—I want to win at everything that I do. The difference today is that there is an obscene amount of pressure to win at every level, and I believe it is ruining the reason most people get involved in sports in the first place.

As for coaches, "If you don't win, you will get fired." That is the ever-present thought in every coach's head in today's world of sports. At every level from the Los Angeles Lakers down to the Division 3 Iowa Wesleyan Tigers in Mount Pleasant, Iowa, the pressure remains—"Win, or you're gone." I believe that pressure and a nasty thing called pride are the two vehicles that drive coaches to become the monsters that we see on sidelines far too often.

I think that coaches have a responsibility and obligation to their players to help them for life after college. Student athletes have four to five years of college, and then they have to be prepared to be successful on their own for the next fifty to sixty. I don't think coaches are unaware of that reality, but I believe they get blinded by the pressure to win and make it more about themselves and less about the players. After all, "If we don't win and I get fired, how am I to going to feed my family?" This is a real fear and struggle for a lot of coaches and I'm afraid we have created a lose-lose situation for coaches everywhere.

Even as a young teenager in high school, this bothered me. We would take the Iowa Test of Basic Skills, and the goal was to "be in the top fortieth percentile" in the state. My mom, being a math teacher at my high school, explained how important those "dumb" standardized tests were for our school to get government funding from the state, etc. "Well that just seems stupid, Mom," I said to her one day before school, as we playfully argued at the kitchen table. "There's no way that everyone in the state can accomplish that, even if everyone is proficient! There's always going to be somebody in the bottom thirty-ninth percentile. This system is set up for people to fail!" I'm sure she probably shook her head and told me to stop being so argumentative and just make sure I do a good job on my test.

That story may seem a bit trivial, but I think the same thing happens in sports today. At most levels in sports, the goal of athletic departments and fans is to win the championship. But there will only be one champion per league at the end of every year. So what happens to the other thousands of teams that didn't accomplish the goal? Does the team who made their post-season tournament for the first time in school history chalk their season up to a failure because they weren't champions? Unfortunately, I think in the last ten years, the solution has become finding someone else who can get the job done and get us to a championship. But where does that philosophy leave us as coaches? Stuck between a rock and a hard place because success is minimized to only winning a championship. I have seen that pressure drive coaches to look at their players as a means to an end, rather than young men and women for whose growth and maturity they are responsible. When the burden to win above all else is put on a coach, they tend to lose sight of what really matters and players become objects. It is a two-way street, though. Fans and administration need to come to the realization that their team isn't going to be the last man standing every year. It's simply not how sports work. So coaches need to have more backbone in sticking to their morals and convictions about the well-being of their athletes. Keeping in mind that producing successful men and women when the ball stops bouncing is more of a reflection on their success as a coach than the number in the left column next their name.

I've learned over the last six years of coaching at the collegiate level that winning is never a guarantee, no matter how well you recruit, how hard you practice, or how prepared you are. There are things that happen that are out of your control each and every year that can make the difference in your team finishing 21-8 or 12-17—injuries, academic issues, illness, bad shooting nights, running into an opponent that is playing well, bad officiating, and the list goes on and on.

If you follow collegiate or professional sports, you will see a "new normal" that has saturated our teams. "If I'm not happy with my current role or satisfaction with the team I'm on, I'll just transfer." In the off-season following the 2017–2018 season, there were over a thousand transfers. That's shocking to me. But when you look at the NBA and see what happens when players aren't happy or not winning the Finals, it starts to make sense. The trickle-down effect of "what to do when you're not happy" is leave.

Winning has become the motivation for all of the decisions that we make in sports today. Players and coaches are merely chess pieces to move around the board of organized sports, and when they stop accomplishing their intended purpose, we need to hit the reset button. What ever happened to sports being a place where people found a sense of family, togetherness, and work ethic? Even though winning is obviously important, I have a hard time believing that a player who is a part of a program that feels loved, appreciated, and supported and is working for something greater than themselves wouldn't stick out the rough waters of college athletics more times than not.

How then do we apply God's Word to the way that we coach? Where do we fit these powerful truths into our program, and in what ways are we missing the mark as a whole? I believe it happens by studying and applying 1 Corinthians 13. I believe God desires for us to step up to the plate and look at these sixteen traits of love, be open and transparent about how they are being mishandled, and search scripture to lead us in our attitudes and actions on a daily basis. These sixteen traits are the road map to how we set ourselves apart from the world and truly reflect what it means to be *the salt of the earth, a city set on a hill.*

If coaching is something that you do for the accolades, fame, or other selfish reasons, attaining those things will never satisfy you. If you have a desire to impact the kingdom of heaven and you believe that God called you to the coaching profession, I believe you are about to go on a journey that could change your life and the lives of every player you coach.

Get ready to discover how to make it to *The Sweet Sixteen*!

Chapter 3

Love Is Patient

"Patience is a virtue." That's what people say, isn't it? It's what parents will say to their child when waiting in a line that doesn't move at the speed that the child would prefer. I hear it said so often by parents to their children that I think it might be in pamphlets that get passed out in delivery rooms. Patience is something that we value as people and do our best to portray as we go through our daily lives, but are we fully aware of what patience looks like? Is something so virtuous as simple as not lashing out in a traffic jam or while waiting in the Starbucks line?

"The capacity to accept or tolerate delay, trouble, or suffering without getting angry or upset." The word "capacity" in this definition of patience is so interesting, because it speaks to there being potential for different levels. The Bible refers to the Holy Spirit in the book of John as the Helper also known as *Parakletos*, meaning "destined to take the place of Christ with the apostles to lead them to a deeper knowledge of the gospel truth, and give them divine strength needed to enable them to undergo trials and persecutions on behalf of the divine kingdom" (BibleStudyTools). How incredible is the definition of the Holy Spirit? His function in our lives, as designed by God, is to come alongside us and empower us to do things that we aren't able to do on our own. As we look at each of *The Sweet Sixteen*, you will see that there are different measures of these traits. In the same way that *agape* is the highest form of love, God desires for us to exhibit the highest capacity of these qualities through the empowering of the Holy Spirit. Each of these characteristics shouldn't follow the status quo of this world, but they should draw people to the Christ within us.

To be patient means that we are required to suffer. The examples I used at the beginning of the chapter spoke to the struggle of delay. We are becoming more and more impatience as a country, and I believe the increase in technology that gets us what we want, when we want it, is partially to blame. Having anything delayed that we anticipate really rubs us the wrong way. But something as powerful as love surely goes beyond being able to wait a few more minutes for something. This is why suffering is also part of patience. There is an assumption at the core of humans that we shouldn't have to suffer, that life should be fair, and that if we haven't done anything wrong, then we shouldn't have any suffering in our lives. I would first like to point out that God's Word says, "In this life you will have trouble. But take heart! I have overcome the world" (John 16:33). As a believer, there is no escaping trouble in this world, but we have the hope that Jesus Christ has overcome. Even still, outside of that life just has a way of dealing us a bad hand from time to time. I'm a firm believer that life is much less about what happens to you, but how you react to it. And it is through these reactions where patience becomes a huge part of life and especially when it comes to coaching.

The game of basketball is hard. For all parties involved, it's hard to ref a perfect game. It's hard to not make bad coaching decisions. It's hard to make all the right plays as a player. This means that patience is huge when it comes to coaching a team, because the number of mistakes that happen in this game will drive someone nuts if they're not patient. I'm not too far removed from my playing days to remember what it's like trying to do everything the coach has instructed you to do, remember the scouting report, and play as hard as you can. I think when players become coaches, it's easy to forget that struggle and not have the necessary patience our players need, just like we did. As a coach, it's so important to understand that everyone learns at different speeds. And on top of that, individuals learn different things at different speeds. Just because a player can recite every word of the scouting report doesn't mean that they can't struggle learning the offense from two different positions.

Early on in my coaching career, I really struggled with this. Whether it was something small, like a particular spacing emphasis, or something more significant like remembering to box out after a shot, I would get extremely irritated when my players would forget time after time. "How many times do I have to tell you?" I would think with a look of disgust on my face and occasionally let out of my mouth. I have come to realize after several years that the answer to that question is as many times as it takes. Well, how many times is that? As many times as it takes. Now, coaches don't like that answer, because it requires this virtue of patience, but the answer still remains the truth. Some people are able to pick up on things and learn quicker than others. What I learned a few years ago is that spending less time being upset and complaining about your team's mistakes and more time considering how to teach differently to help them learn is much more efficient—it requires you to be a great coach! Lots of people are able to diagnose a symptom, but doctors get paid the big bucks because they know how to cure it.

One very common area of frustration for coaches is during practice, when players aren't performing well. Whether it's their execution, their lack of energy, or their inability to remember what coach has taught, it all tests the patience of a coach. The struggle that we all as coaches face is wanting things to be done the way we want them done and dealing with our expectations not being met. There could be dozens of reasons why players fall short of expectations, but the thing that I believe is most valuable to the health of the team is allowing players to be human, meaning you give them grace, and space, to make mistakes, have bad practices, and fail to execute here and there. As I said earlier, the game of basketball is hard! There are very few players who intentionally set out to make mistakes. They want to do things right and make you proud as a coach, but excellence takes time and patience.

I think it's important to recognize the difference between making tactical mistakes, and effort mistakes, and how to handle them differently. If a player is consistently making tactical mistakes, I believe you need to make a judgment call on whether their potential is worth the repetition required to help them figure it out. If the answer is yes, then you should stick with it and be patient. If the answer is no, then you can simply stop playing them. In both cases, the need to yell and scream isn't necessary. If the mistakes are effort mistakes, it's important to find out if they know what your standard of effort is. If they know the standard and choose not to live up to it, they shouldn't be playing regardless of who they are. If the player truly wants to play, they will raise their level of intensity to meet the standard. In a situation where effort is the problem, I think it's important to let the player know that is the reason they aren't playing so they don't attribute it to something other than their effort.

Instead of *ripping into* a kid for forgetting what to do on a particular play, *speak* to them. You can convey the exact same message and disappointment with their lack of focus by talking to them as you can when you scream. You can even punish them, but yelling at them isn't a requirement for behavior modification. When your team starts a practice with a clear lack of energy, or they don't seem to really care to be there, try stopping the practice and tell your captains/upperclassmen to address the team, instead of feeling like the threat of punishment is the best way to light a fire in them. Sometimes players are motivated more by their own teammates than by a coach, and at the same time, you can help your captains develop their leadership skills. If players continue to mess something up—whether it's a ball-screen coverage, a technique in post defense, or anything that you want done a certain way—instead of talking down to them about how bad they are at that skill, find a new way to explain it so they understand better or, and this is where the test of patience comes in, just continue to calmly teach and reiterate what it is that you want without getting upset.

As coaches, we are teachers. It is our responsibility to use our God-given ability of teaching to figure out how each one of our players learns and meet them there. For some players, they need to do something thirty times correctly before it clicks. For others, they need to see themselves on film to make the connection between what you want and how they're doing it differently. Others might simply need you to explain it better or differently. Regardless of the learning style, take pride in your gift of teaching, and learn how to grow *with* your players! The reward is that once you discover how each player learns, you can be more effective in your teaching methods moving forward.

The second part of the definition of patience addressed the idea of suffering. A huge part of the game where coaches deal with suffering is in the area of losing. As I talked about before, coaches are under pressure to win for the security of their future employment. A coach who is preparing for their first games of the season is extremely susceptible to losing patience with their players when they feel they aren't playing at the level necessary to be successful. It's important to keep in mind that our players have thoughts, feelings, and emotions as well. A coach is not the only person on a team that gets anxious about whether the team will be successful or not. Players are smart enough to know when the team "isn't quite there yet." That means it's imperative as a coach that you encourage your players and fill them with confidence. Let them know you are in their corner and believe in them. After all, there are thousands of talented players in the world and dozens of ways to strategically win a basketball game. There are very few substitutes for confidence.

Another area where your patience will be tested is when it comes to team standards. Having a set of standards on a team is so important for a coach. There should be a clear set of rules and guidelines that your team knows they are required to live up to. Young adults, more times than not, rise to the standards that are set for them when they are enforced and modeled by their coach. I've seen some programs where standards are set very low because the coach doesn't want to deal with the potential of their players breaking these guidelines and having to sit out. The motivation behind this goes back to coaches selfishly being more concerned with players being able to win games than growing into quality men and women, even if it means losing a few games in the process. When a coach is trying to create, or sustain, a culture of excellence in their program and some of their players decide to push the boundaries, it is extremely difficult to be patient in your discipline and stick to your standards. Knowing that you could lose a few (or a lot of) games while the players sit out is a test of patience that coaches really struggle to ride out. In both situations of dealing with poor performance and bad behavior, a coach's character is put on center stage to be examined. Do they fight the urge to put the blame on the players for not performing? Or do they find a different way to help them learn what they're trying to teach? Do they truly stand by their convictions and standards of excellence regardless of who breaks the rules?

If you have a certain rule on your team that you believe in, and is for the betterment of your player's maturity, and one, or more, of your players is defiant toward that rule, be consistent. I believe it is the nature of mankind to push the boundaries of authority. Toddlers learn this very quickly. "If I scream in the checkout isle of Target long enough, dad will buy me this candy bar, just to shut me up." "If mommy tells me I'm not getting up from the table until I finish my broccoli and I'm stubborn long enough, she'll cave and let me throw it away." If we learn this disobedient behavior as kids, why would we assume that same thought process doesn't still exist as young adults?

This is why you must have strong convictions about the rules, standards, and guidelines for your team, because when players don't live up to the standards, it's important that you believe in them, rather than allowing your lines to move. And when a player, regardless of how good they are, decides to break those guidelines, the consequence needs to be consistent. I know as coaches, and even as parents, we will get tired of being consistent with our consequences. Thoughts of doubting if that players will ever change will most likely flood your mind. This is where we have to be patient! We must trust the process of the relationship that we have with our players and know that our patience will reap a harvest of obedience, if we don't give up.

Love requires us to exhibit patience, not only when it's easy but also when it's hard! When the ramifications of your patience test the deepest part of your character is when you find out how much you truly love your players. I believe that God ordered *The Sweet Sixteen* with thoughtfulness and intentionality. If we are able to get ahold of patience in our daily lives as a coach, I think it creates a foundation for the rest of the traits to build upon. With each one of these chapters, my desire is we examine ourselves with honesty and humility and ask ourselves if we love our players in these ways.

I want you to know that this process of love is not a destination, but a journey. It's difficult, and you are going to have struggles and failures intertwined in your victories. It's the pursuit of excellence that brings God joy, as He strengthens you on your daily walk with Him. You need to be prepared to deal with taking steps backward and asking God to forgive you and help you grow. To this point in my coaching career, I have had a lot of success in the area of patience when I am on the sidelines, but I really struggle with it when I play. I am lucky to still be healthy enough in my late twenties to practice with our team and play pickup basketball in my free time. But it is amazing how my patience vanishes into thin air the moment I am inside the lines.

This is an area that God is working on me daily that has been a struggle since college. There's something about the fear of losing when I have a physical part in the outcome that turns me into a person that I honestly don't like. I yell at my teammates when they screw something up. I get very upset when fouls are called against me unjustly or a player fouls me and doesn't call it. Between the eye-rolling, covering my face with my shirt in frustration, and regularly scheduled arguing, I'm surprised people want to play on my team sometimes. I am so consumed with not only winning but also playing without mistakes that I act in a way that I know isn't glorifying to God. It actually ruins the entire experience sometimes, even when I play well and we win. I've had days where I leave the gym so disappointed with my behavior, because I acted like an idiot for two hours in front of guys that I know I'm called to be an example of Christ toward.

I think it's important for you to know that God wants all of you. He isn't satisfied with some behavior modification that makes people think, "You're not as much of a jerk as you used to be." He wants every area of your life to be an opportunity for His love to shine through your actions, and I'll be the first one to admit I'm nowhere close to that. In a lot of ways, it's just like coaching. Your offense can be playing at a high level, but you can't guard anyone. Or you'll have found a lot of success getting to the basket, but now you can't make any free throws. Getting every facet of the game where you want it seems impossible, and managing these sixteen characteristics to your players will feel like that too. For whatever reason, I'm able to control my frustration when I'm coaching, but I really struggle when it comes to playing the game. If you're truly ready to commit to being a *Sweet Sixteen* coach, you are going to have to be very humble and transparent with yourself about where you're at with each of these traits. My desire is to be honest with you in the areas I struggle, in hopes that seeing my flaws will help you address yours. "And let us consider how we may spur one another on toward love and good deeds" (Hebrews 10:24, NIV).

The Bible speaks a lot about patience. Here are some scriptures that you can read, write down, and meditate on to help you show *agape* to your players through patience.

> Be always humble, gentle, and patient. Show your love by being tolerant with one another. (Ephesians 4:2)

> Hot tempers cause arguments, but patience brings peace. (Proverbs 15:18)

> The end of something is better than its beginning. Patience is better than pride. (Ecclesiastes 7:8)

> Whoever is patient has great understanding, but one who is quick-tempered displays folly. (Proverbs 14:29)

> Be joyful in hope, patient in affliction, faithful in prayer. (Romans 12:12)

> Better a patient person than a warrior, one with self-control than one who takes a city. (Proverbs 16:32)

Be still before the Lord and wait patiently for him; do not fret when people succeed in their ways, when they carry out their wicked schemes. (Psalms 37:7)

Chapter 4

Love Is Kind

Kindness—what an undervalued quality in people today, not just coaches. Whether it's manifested in bullying, racial prejudice, or Internet trolling, our world is full of people who lack kindness. The songs that get played on the radio far too often are disrespectful to someone. The next time you see a meme, however funny it may be, ask yourself if it's kind toward the person it's intended for. We praise people like Danielle Bregoli and make them famous because of their disrespect. And to prove my point, most of you reading this don't know that name, but will connect the dots when you find out she is the teenager, made famous on Dr. Phil for the line she said to her mother, "Catch me outside, how 'bout dat?" The desire to be kind to one another is decreasing all around us, which ultimately means that we are failing to love one another more and more.

Kindness and competition could probably be considered oxymoron in today's sports culture. The next time you're at a game, take some time and listen to the things that get said to referees. Listen to what fans says to the opposing team. Worst of all, the next time you see a coach verbally accosting an official for making a call they disagree with, listen for the cheers of support the coach gets from their fans. It's really sad when you remove yourself from the intensity of the game and realize that a group of people are cheering on a person screaming at another person in disgust. It is the epitome of what kindness is not. And unfortunately, sports have a way of bringing that out in people.

Think back to the opening story of the book. Think about the emotions that arose in your heart as you pictured the scene playing out as if you were sitting there in the arena watching it happen. My assumption is that most of you were heartbroken, upset, angry, or maybe even sick to your stomach at the thought of this happening. Yet most of us are so quick to scream at an official when we feel they've missed a call or made one that we disagree with. Whether we want to admit it or not, and I am putting myself in this category as well, we are hypocritical when it comes to kindness. As quickly as we are able to call it out in someone else, we exhibit the same behavior when we feel it's warranted.

This is why God's Word is so powerful. 1 Corinthians 1:27 says, "But God chose the foolish things of this world to shame the wise." Real love is going to challenge you to act in a way that isn't always going to be popular. The truth is most of the time if you want to be in step with God, it means you're going to be out of step with society. To most people, the idea of not yelling at referees and not talking trash about the opponents is stupid, it's soft, and it means you're not invested in your team's success or wanting to win. If what the Bible says goes against what's popular in today's culture, that's all the confirmation that you need to know it's going to bring you success in life. When you find yourself swimming upstream for the sake of God's Word, you're definitely on course. The problem is most people would rather be comfortable than obedient, because true kindness must be an action, not a reaction. "I'll be respectful to the refs when they do their job better," is not kindness. "I wasn't going to run my mouth until the other team's coach started talkin' trash," is a reaction. It puts your obedience in subjection to other people doing it first. That's not love.

The irony is in what the last half of 1 Corinthians 1:27 says, "God chose the weak things of the world to put to shame the strong." God tells us that what the world calls tough will be put to shame by the weak. The fact that most people who say that it's soft to not yell at the refs or try to intimidate the opponent is the very evidence that it's actually what God calls wise and powerful!

Coaches have such a profound impact on the kindness that is exhibited in their program. They lead the charge in the direction that their players grow in maturity. The number of times I have heard a coach say to the team, "Don't yell at the refs. That's my job," is too many to count. What example is that setting for their players? That there is a certain position that you can attain where you graduate from the expectation of being kind? It's a model that players learn from and typically end up repeating, because guess what most of the irate dads in the stands at games were doing during their teenage years? Most likely observing their coach say the same things they now say from the bleachers, as a parent. And in a lot of relationships, the husband demonstrates this type of behavior enough that the wife begins to act the same way. If a player sees their coach acting this way, then they look up in the stands and see their parents doing the same thing, it's almost inevitable that they will think it's appropriate later in life. The vicious cycle will continue. The coach's influence has a ripple effect that stretches far past what the eye can see. It's so important that we recognize that and set a great example with our influence.

The relationship between coach and player is another area where kindness has been lost in coaching. In a game where a player's confidence is such a valuable and delicate thing, coaches can have a way of pruning it down to nothing with their negativity. In terms of looking at "the glass as half empty or half full," it typically tends to look "half empty" to coaches.

Proverbs 18:21 says, "The tongue can bring death or life; those who love to talk will reap the consequences." Coaches have the ability to alter the course of their player's lives by what they choose to say to them. In basketball, there are always things that can be improved on, but at the same time, there are usually things that are worthy of praise. What a coach chooses to magnify is typically what a player thinks and believes about themselves. If this is the truth, we should be *eager* to speak encouragement and life into our players, understanding that we have a direct correlation to their success and understanding we will reap benefits far greater and far beyond what we reap when we sow negativity.

If a player is doing something well, praise them for it, give life to their soul, and help them know that you recognize what they do well. If a player is struggling in an area, there is something powerful about having the ability to call it out, but doing it in kindness. The old expression, "sticks and stones may break my bones, but words can never hurt me," couldn't be any further from the truth because the truth is in God's Word and He says that your words have a profound impact on the people who hear them. This can be proven. If you have a chance to be around a team where the coach is always saying unkind things to the players and his negativity far outweighs his compliments, watch how that team performs. More importantly, see if you can hear what the players talk about. My prediction is that it will reflect what gets spoken into them the most. If a player is struggling to make free throws and their coach is always reminding them of it, watch their demeanor when they step to the free throw line. The worry, doubt, and lack of confidence almost seep out of their pores. They aren't thinking about making the shot; they're thinking about what happens if they don't.

The verse in Proverbs ends with, "Those who love to talk will reap the consequences." Sports are an excellent place to see God's Word come to life. When a coach finds things that are praiseworthy and lets their team know it and is kind and gracious in correction, players are confident. They tend to trust themselves, because they know their coach is confident in them, and the coach reaps the fruit of his words.

I remember having a player that I coached who was a post player. He was a big dude with big-time athletic ability. He didn't know how good he could be if he simplified his game and just focused on doing a couple of things really well. He struggled a lot, because he was constantly trying to do things that he quite frankly shouldn't be doing. I had the hardest time getting him to roll to the basket when he set screens, because he wanted to pick and pop and shoot jumpers. At the time, I was playing a lot in practice, as the scout team point guard, so I was on the court with him. I put my arm around him and looked him in the eyes and said, "Dive straight to the rim after you set that ball screen and I PROMISE you'll be open, and I'll get it to you. Just trust me." After a few trips up and down the court, he came and set a ball screen for me and dove to the rim. I took a couple of bounces, looked off the help defender, and fired a pass to him. He caught that thing and about ripped the rim off when he dunked it! It was awesome, and I was hyped. He turned and looked at me right after coming down off the rim with a huge smile on his face.

I ran over to him and said, "Bro, if you do that every time, you'll score that easy a lot."

Still smiling, he said, "I got you, Coach!"

In case you're wondering, he rolled every single time the rest of the day and had a lot of success doing so.

I could have easily yelled at him and told him that he was an awful shooter and had no business popping after his screen, because he was never going to make it—because the truth is he probably would have missed ten to fifteen of those shots before he ever made one. If I would have told him how bad of a shooter he was, it wouldn't have been a lie, but I bet he would have spent the rest of practice thinking about how mad he was that coach told him he was a bad shooter. By thinking about what would be beneficial and uplifting to him, I chose to magnify what he is good at rather than focus on what he's not good at. I convinced him that rolling will help him be more successful and asked him to trust me, and the results speak for themselves.

I challenge every coach who reads this to be intentional about finding the self-control to think before you speak to your players. Don't react out of frustration and "let the chips fall where they may." Be intentional with the words that you speak, knowing that there is the potential for life and death in them. Be intentional about looking for things to praise your players for, and when you do need to correct them, do it with the motive of kindness. The Bible says in Ephesians 4:15 to "speak the truth in love," and this should be our goal. We don't want to ignore the mistakes or lie to keep from saying something mean. We do, however, need to find a way to be honest and do it with the intention of encouraging them through the process. This is where the foundation of patience can come alongside you and help you consistently show kindness even when you want to lose your temper. Let's work on showing our players kindness in their struggles, when they need it most, to give them the strength to keep grinding.

Finally, kindness needs to be applied to the way players treat one another. I'm very well aware of the things that are commonly said on the basketball court from one team to another, and it's not great. I'm also aware of the belief that one of the best ways to beat your opponent is to intimidate them. I won't even argue that it doesn't work, because I think it does give your team an edge. However, the number one goal of our lives shouldn't be to win basketball games—it should be to reflect the indescribable love of God to everyone you have the opportunity to be around. Yes, that means your opponent as well. Sports give believers an incredible opportunity to spread God's love to people, because (1) sports are typically played in front of large crowds; (2) it's assumed that players are going to do whatever they have to so they can be crowned the victor, even if it's frowned upon; and (3) the high standard the Bible calls us to live up to stands out in sports more than most other events in life.

Being both a Division 1 basketball and football player, I have heard and seen almost everything imaginable through taunting or talking trash. I even struggle to keep my mouth free of disrespectful comments when I play. It's a very enticing thing to get caught up in, especially when your opponent engages in it with you. I'm sure some people would even write it off as being "harmless" or "a part of the game." My question is, is it a part of the kingdom? That has to be the question that you ask yourself when you judge your speech during sports. I'm not saying this is easy! It's actually incredibly difficult. James 3:2 says, "We all stumble in many ways. Anyone who is never at fault in what they say is perfect, able to keep their whole body in check." Wow! What a statement. It's hard to believe that a person could be perfect, and what's even more shocking is that God's Word says controlling what you say is the key element to doing so.

Our tongues are vicious, and because of the competitiveness that is revealed in sports, we tend to let our words run wild when we are trying to win. Our mouth can become like a hungry Rottweiler that's been freed from its collar, looking to rip into anything it can get its paws on, at the first sign of weakness. The worst part about trash-talking is that it typically doesn't stop with one person. It brings everyone in earshot along for the ride, and before you know it, the calmest-tempered people start to join in. There is never an excuse or loophole to disrespect other people. This is what separates love from its counterfeit. When love is just a feeling, it makes sense to say a few explicit words to the other team when they had it coming. When we allow *agape* to rule in our hearts, we make the choice to keep our mouth shut so God can be glorified by our kindness in the face of disrespect.

What a great way to teach your team how to truly love. By making it a standard that disrespect and trash-talking will not be a part of how your team plays, then you can compete with tenacity and not tear down your opponent in the process. Because kindness is so rare in sports, it is a great way to set your team apart from most by excelling in kindness. Make no mistake, this doesn't mean you're forfeiting being a hard-nosed team that makes their presence known. It just means that you don't need to taint your success with rudeness toward people that Jesus died for.

In order to do this, I think you must be a living example of kindness before you can call your players to rise to that standard. One of the things I love about coaching is that we have to first be the example of what we want our players to be. We need to exhibit kindness on a daily basis so our team understands what it looks like, and they know that we don't just talk the talk, but we walk the walk. Then I believe we should challenge our players to treat one another, and the opponents, with kindness even when we don't feel like it. This won't be easy, and it will most likely take patience due to the strong pull in all of us to say things out of emotion. But it's possible, if we are willing to put the time in and rely on God's help for strength.

The Bible gives us such a wonderful example of kindness by how God continues to show us grace and mercy, even when we don't deserve it. In our mess, our sins, and our shortcomings, God shows us kindness time after time. I find it very applicable, because it's not based on how good we are, but on how kind He is. These verses will hopefully spur you on toward kindness, by remembering how kind your heavenly Father has been to you.

> But when the kindness and love of God our Savior appeared, He saved us, not because of righteous things we had done, but because of His mercy. He saved us through the washing of rebirth and renewal by the Holy Spirit, whom He poured out on us generously through Jesus Christ our Savior, so that, having been justified by His grace, we might become heirs having the hope of eternal life. (Titus 3:4–7)

> Therefore, as God's chosen people, holy and dearly loved, clothe yourselves with compassion, kindness, humility, gentleness and patience. (Colossians 3:12)

> Be kind to one another, tenderhearted, forgiving one another, as God in Christ forgave you. (Ephesians 4:32)

> But the fruit of the Spirit is love, joy peace, patience, kindness, goodness faithfulness, gentleness, and self-control. There is no law against these things! (Galatians 5:22–23)

> Whoever pursues righteousness and kindness will find life, righteousness, and honor. (Proverbs 21:21)

Chapter 5

It Does Not Envy

"Green isn't a good color on you." That's the expression that our society uses to implicate someone for being jealous of something or someone else. To be "green with envy" is a trait that we are all aware is a poor one to exhibit. The Merriam-Webster dictionary defines envy as painful or resentful awareness of an advantage enjoyed by another joined with a desire to possess the same advantage. The last of the Ten Commandments is do not covet. God knows that His creation is susceptible to seeing what other people have and wanting it for themselves, so He strictly forbids us from allowing those desires to motivate us. And at the very root of humanity, we recognize the problem involved in being envious, but we still struggle to control its appeal.

Doesn't it seem natural to want the good things that other people have? Wouldn't it make sense to see the advantages that other people have been given and want them for yourself? On the surface, it seems harmless to want to be like someone else or have what they have. But when you look deeper, the problem with wanting what someone else has is when we begin to believe that if we just had what "they" had, we would be satisfied. The error in believing this is that the only thing in this world that can truly sustain you is being in a relationship with God. More money, more trophies, higher status, and more material possessions might make you feel good but they will never sustain you—they weren't designed to fulfill you. It's why you see celebrities with "everything," and they seem just as anxious, depressed, and suicidal as people that don't have anything. When we spend our time always chasing after what we don't have, we get caught in the trap of never feeling like we have enough. Once you finally get that raise in salary, the immediate happiness is quickly replaced with the drive to want the next one. If the school finally increases your budget, it will make you happy until you find out that another team in your conference still has more than you. Ladies, the designer bag or name brand leggings might seem like the thing standing between you and the self-confidence that you're searching for, but there will always be a newer outfit and another friend who has something you don't. Greed and envy deceive us into believing that the next "thing" is the thing that will bring you joy.

Consider the implications of being envious of someone else because of the gifts and talents that they have. At the root of that envy, we are ultimately believing that God made a mistake when He created us. Jeremiah 29:11 says, "'For I know the plans I have for you,' says the Lord. 'They are plans for good and not for disaster, to give you a future and a hope.'" If we believe that God created us with a specific plan and purpose, then we must believe that God put everything necessary to fulfill His good and perfect will for our lives, inside of us. To look at the gifts and talents of other people and think it's not fair is to say that God didn't equip you with the talents necessary to accomplish His plan for you. Part of our faith in God is believing that not only were our abilities given to us for God's pleasure, but also we have *everything* we need to be exactly who God called us to be.

I really struggled with this once I got to Iowa State. After three semesters of junior college, I had finally gotten to the place I'd spent my entire life grinding toward—Division 1. It hit me hard when I finally got there and realized that the athletic ability that was required to be successful at that elite level was something I didn't have. And if I did have it, I grew up in such a small town that I didn't have the resources available to develop it early enough. It was really hard to deal with and accept. *It's not fair!* I thought quite often. *If I were 6'4", I guarantee you I would be starting instead of riding the bench.* Feelings of jealously and frustration hit me hard during that three-year period of my life. Even though I loved my teammates and experience as a Cyclone and even though I believe God showed me favor in the route that got me there, it came with a lot of disappointment. The biggest reason that I was so frustrated was because I felt I was always called to play professionally, and for the first time in my life, there was a clear indicator that it probably wasn't going to happen. In my discouragement, God was so faithful in stirring up in my heart the passion for coaching, as the dream of playing professionally was dying. He never left me alone in the "wilderness" of young adulthood, not knowing what my purpose was.

What I want to illuminate in my story is that it was up to me to listen to God and be obedient to His calling for <u>my</u> life. I could have continued to magnify the bitterness I had about my lack of ability. I could have chosen to think that God "did me dirty" by not giving me the height, quickness, or athletic ability that my teammates had. I could have stayed envious of all the abilities of my teammates that played over me. But God had never abandoned me in my entire life. He never gave me a reason not to trust Him, and I can confidently say that I find more joy from coaching basketball than I ever did playing it. What is even more incredible about my testimony is the reason I can coach the way I do is because of the countless hours I spent focusing on every detail of the game to close the gap between me and the players who were more talented than I was. God used my drive to do "the impossible" as a player to help me be an excellent coach, because I know how to see the smallest details of the game now. That skill was learned during those years of pursuing my dream of playing professionally, and I doubt I would have been committed to do that if I knew the NBA was never in the cards. Isaiah 55:8–9 says, "'For my thoughts are not your thoughts, neither are your ways my ways,' declares the Lord. 'As the heavens are higher than the earth, so are my ways higher than your ways and my thoughts than your thoughts.'" I am a living testimony of this scripture. God knows you better than you will ever know yourself, because He formed every facet of your being together for His good pleasure. Trust Him and believe that He gave you everything that you need to fulfill His will for your life and that it will bring you more joy than anything that you could ever make happen for yourself.

How then is envy revealed in coaching? I'm glad you asked. One of the things I am around a lot as a coach is complaining. It's hard to spend a considerable amount of time with coaches and not find the conversation head down a path of complaining about what their school doesn't have or what other schools do have that makes it impossible to compete with them. Because of the constant thoughts of winning that are always on the mind of a coach, it's very easy to find reasons why it's so hard to do so. And very similar to what we talked about in regard to people trash-talking in chapter 5 and how it typically isn't just one person involved, once one coach starts to talk about what they lack, it spreads like wildfire to everyone in the conversation.

Coaches need to accept the fact that there will most likely never be a time in their life when everything meets a hundred percent of their expectations. I don't think there will ever be a team, university, or program where there aren't things to complain about. It's a part of life, because life isn't fair. If you set out to find all the areas of inequality, you will never stop finding them. The best coaches are the ones who take what they do have and make the best out of what they have.

As a coach, athletic director, parent, or player, it is incredibly important that you set the example of not being envious of other programs, players, and facilities that aren't yours. And you do this with your language day in and day out. This seems really simple, but after reading this chapter, you will start to see how quickly conversations can go south in the direction of jealously and comparison. Your players pick up on the things you complain about. Now, I'm not saying that coaches shouldn't look at the teams that are successful at their level and learn from the success of other programs; I actually think that's incredibly wise. But there is a difference between trying to grow as a program and wanting to find things to give you an excuse for why you're not able to be better.

Coaches tell their players, "Play through it," when things don't go the way they planned or adversity hits during practice and games. A coach wants to see their players have the mental toughness to not get hung up on a mistake, or bad call, and focus on what they can do to turn it around. I think that coaches need to "play through it" in regard to things that other programs have that they don't. If you, as a coach, don't dwell on the things that you can't control outside your program, it will be that much easier to tell your players that regardless of what happens during a game, "we play through it."

In the same way that I struggled with comparison when I was in college, a lot of players have a hard time dealing with being envious of other players—not only the players on their team but also players on other teams. This issue can be detrimental to the success of your team. There is a portion of scripture that explains the function of the body of Christ and the mind-set we are to have as believers and brothers and sisters in Christ. I think it creates a parallel with the teams that we coach and how we can teach our players how important each and every one of them are to the success of the program.

> Yes, the body has many different parts, not just one part. If the foot says, "I am not a part of the body because I am not a hand," that does not make it any less a part of the body. And if the ear says, "I am not part of the body because I am not an eye," would that make it any less a part of the body? If the whole body were an eye, how would you hear? Or if your whole body were an ear, how would you smell anything?
>
> But our bodies have many parts, and God has put each part just where he wants it. How strange a body would be if it had only one part! Yes, there are many parts, but only one body. The eye can never say to the hand, "I don't need you." The head can't say to the feet, "I don't need you."
>
> In fact, some parts of the body that seem weakest and least important are actually the most necessary. And the parts we regard as less honorable are those we clothe with the greatest care. So we carefully protect those parts that should not

be seen, while the more honorable parts do not require this special care. So God has put the body together such that extra honor and care are given to those parts that have less dignity. This makes for harmony among the members, so that all the members care for each other. If one part suffers, all the parts suffer with it, and if one part is honored, all the parts are glad. All of you together are Christ's body, and each of you is a part of it. (1 Corinthians 12:14–27)

Just like a body has many different parts and each one of those parts is valuable to the proper functioning of the body, the same is true for a team. There is so much value in a head coach communicating this to their team and explaining how each person fits into the big picture. When each player doesn't understand the value that they bring, it's very common to find individuals on a team being envious of their teammates, because they don't know their worth (much like verses 15 and 16). This understanding of each member being unique and important starts at the top and goes all the way down to the last player on the bench.

Head Coach (The Head)

The Bible uses the word headship in regard to marriage and family, meaning leadership and authority. A team is very much like a family, and the head coach is very much like the father of that team. Not only are they responsible for the decisions that are made on the team, but also they have to take responsibility for the actions that are made by any other part of the body. The head sets the direction of the entire body, and the body is a reflection of how healthy the head, or headship, is. While the head gets to be in charge and make decisions, it also holds the largest amount of scrutiny and accountability. The healthy relationship between the head and the body is a two-way street. The head must give direction and instill purpose into each member of the body, and the body, in return, needs to give honor and respect to the headship. Lastly, it is critical that every head coach be under the authority of someone else. Typically, that would be an athletic director or principal/chancellor/provost. The need for a head to be under authority is because God calls everyone to submit to Him, and having an earthly authority that we submit to gives us an example to learn from. It also gives the body an example of what it looks like to honor authority. The players understand what it means to respect the head coach, as they see the head coach respect the people over them.

Assistant Coach (The Neck)

The assistants are the neck because they support the head, and they are an extension of the head to the rest of the body. They play a unique role, because they are not the final authority, but they do have some authority on the team. They often are the go-between who can see both sides of the coin and have more personal relationships with the players than the head coach does. They typically are doing a lot of the work that has to be done after it is delegated to them by the head coach. They typically spend more time watching tape and preparing for the next game than anyone else, which means they may know more about how to win than anyone. They also hold a huge role in wearing multiple hats as far as recruiting, playing in practice, doing scouting reports, holding study hall hours, running drills in practice, etc. They are responsible for covering the blind spots of the head coach, making sure the head coach is freed up to lead. As an assistant, it's important to understand how valuable all the things that you do are for the success of your team. They might go unnoticed and underappreciated, but the team would not be the same without you.

Star Player (The Arms)

The arms draw attention. When an athlete has arms that are defined and sculpted, people recognize them. Our generation of young men spend hours sculpting them in the local gym, and young ladies long to have theirs be toned. Because of the recognition that the arms get, most people spend a lot of time and energy making theirs look impressive. They are valuable in almost every sport that exists, but it's important to remember that arms without legs or a core wouldn't be very useful, much like a star player wouldn't be very successful without a strong team around them. It's no secret that every player dreams of being the star on a team. Everyone wants to be the person with the ball in their hands at the end of the game and the pressure on them. A lot of current coaches used to be that person when they played. This position is not an easy one, and with the fame and popularity comes a lot of criticism. These players have to put in more work than most, because they have an expectation of their game being at an elite level every day. They typically are asked to play through injuries, sickness, and personal issues that happen during the course of a season. Not everyone has the capacity, or the ability, to be one of the stars, and too many players try to be one when they're not. There is an obvious gifting that has been given to "star players" that can't be manufactured. Either you have it or you don't. If you have it, it's important that you work on your gift and get the most out of it. It's equally as important that you remember that the gift was given to you to bring glory back to the Giver. Don't let your talent be something you use to promote yourself. It's also important to remember to honor and praise your teammates for the role that they play. With the exception of a few sports, nobody can win all by themselves. Give credit to the teammates who make a way for your gift to shine.

Role Player (The Core)

The core is often overlooked because it is typically covered up. Not only can it be overlooked, but also its purpose of connecting and supporting the strength of our four limbs can go unrecognized. The core is more than just washboard abs. It is the centerpiece of your body working properly. If your core is weak, you will most likely experience back pain. If you have incredibly strong legs and the natural ability to sprint fast but you have a weak core, you won't get the most out of your leg strength. The core holds the body together and enhances the performance of all the other main muscle groups. Your core literally makes the easy task of standing up straight possible. Role players hold the same function on a team. The players who do the things that aren't going to be on highlights from a game are incredibly valuable. They are the players that truly win you games. I played football at the Division 1 level and spent a ton of time reading about my favorite QB Drew Brees. I read how much value he placed on his offensive linemen, how he would take them out to dinner regularly, how he would praise them in post-game interviews, and how he always made them feel important. Most people wouldn't be able to tell you any of the linemen's stats or possibly what their first names were. Linemen don't get a lot of screen time or highlights centered around their play, because it's not flashy. However, you cannot win a football game with a bad line. They determine which team has the advantage the entire game. Their value far outweighs their recognition. It's the same for the undersized power forward on the team that gets three offensive rebounds every game and only shoots open layups. The same is true for the guy who takes pride in guarding the other team's best offensive player the entire night. Great teams need a "core group of guys" who are willing to do the little things to make a team successful. When a coach finds a player who isn't necessarily a great scorer but has a lot of intangibles, it would be wise of them to find ways to get the most out of that player.

Bench Player/Walk-On (The Legs)

The legs are the foundation of the body. They help us move and create opportunities for the arms to do all that they are capable of doing. It's easy to neglect our legs, because they're not the flashy muscles, and they usually require more maintenance when you spend time developing them. If you're going to dedicate yourself to gaining strength in your legs, you're going to have to spend time stretching, foam rolling, and training through soreness. However, the best athletes in every sport are the ones who have great leg strength. Developing strong legs is something that you might not think is a big deal if they're weak, but you notice a huge difference in your abilities after you've strengthened them. The same is true for a team in regard to the players that don't play a lot. Lots of teams get by and are even successful with very few players or a bad group of bench players. But if you look at the championship teams that win year in and year out, they have guys who don't play very much that take their role very seriously. There is so much that goes into being successful, besides for the game itself, that people don't realize. As a former practice player and scout team guy, I knew how valuable my role was in preparing the team for game day. The preparation and scouting that goes into preparing for each opponent is crucial to winning consistently. Having quality players who run the scout team and prepare the team for the next opponent really shows come game time. It's easy to forget about the scout team, but when those players are locked in, they help your entire practice be the most efficient it can be. Not to mention, your scout team has to, in some ways, be smarter than your starters. They are asked to learn a new team's plays every week and run them with precision. I think it's vital that you encourage these players to work hard and you let them know how important their role is to the team's success. The more talented your scout team is, the better competition your starters are going to get in practice. Lastly, if you have talented players who you think may have a chance to be in a bigger role later in their career, the scout team is a great place for them to compete against your best players and grow their basketball IQ in the process.

It is imperative that your players know why they are valuable and have a profound impact to the team, regardless of what part they play. One of the most important elements to a championship team is getting everyone bought in to the goal of winning and knowing and accepting their role in the pursuit. Second, it's important for every member of the team to support and honor each person on the team for the role they play, no matter how big or small. This is one of the most difficult things to achieve in sports because of the desire to be "the star." This championship environment is created when a coach puts value on each individual and makes sure they know how important they are to the overall success of the team. Too many teams today have players that believe because they're not a starter or because they only score five points per game or because they are just a scout team player, then they don't matter. A team needs all those players giving the team their best effort for the team to be successful. In fact, if you go back and read 1 Corinthians starting at verse 22, you will see a very strange command. He says that we are actually supposed to give more care and honor to the parts that are unseen than the parts that are seen. The reason for this is revealed in verse 25 when he says, "This makes for harmony among the members, so that all the members care for each other." As a coach, it is so important that the players who play the most and receive the most attention recognize and honor the players who are unseen. If you want a team that cares for one another, I believe this is the way to do it. This comes from you setting that example first and foremost. You should go out of your way to give honor to the people that the media and the fans tend to forget about. Your starters will begin to truly care about the players at the end of the bench, and the bench players will be compelled to work that much harder to help the starters be prepared for game day.

After making sure each player understands their role on the team, it's important to encourage them as they do their job. It's easy to only focus on the top players on your team once the season is in full swing. But just like 1 Corinthians 12 teaches us, if we begin to neglect certain parts of the body, the whole body starts to suffer. If everyone on the team was a starter, who would they play against in practice in preparation for games? If everyone was the scorer on the team, who would pass the ball? If everyone was the shooter on the team, who would set screens to get the shooters open? A team needs every part to be successful. But more importantly, a team needs everyone to know how important their part is. Deep down, I think people want to be a part of something bigger than themselves. What better way to help your team rise above the struggle of envy than by being empowered and bought in to how important their role is?

A unique thing about sports is that each year, players graduate and leave the program, which means there are new roles available each year for players to fill. One thing that I see happen far too often is a player in a role that they don't prefer uses their time to slack off and complain about the role they are in rather than work diligently to be the best they can be. I see this happen with freshman and sophomores a lot. They think they deserve to be the star or starter, so they neglect working on their craft, and when a new season rolls around, they haven't put in the work to qualify themselves for a new role. They become more bitter and do less, which affirms the coach's decision to put someone else in the role that they might have had planned for the player who wasted their time. It's a horrible reality that I believe can be overcome by a coach reminding their players how valuable their *current* role is and how important it is to work every day to be the best they can be.

This lesson is one we can teach in sports, because we see how beneficial it is for the programs that have it embedded in their culture. But more importantly, we need to teach this to our players as it pertains to life outside of sports. God has designed each and every person with a specific role on "His team" to advance the kingdom of God on this earth. Each one of us has been given everything we need to be effective and successful in His plan for us. As a coach, we can demonstrate the parallels of the kingdom by reminding our players of their significance in our team's success, but I want to see coaches rise up in sports and teach their players how significant they are in God's team. I want coaches to encourage, equip, and empower their players to know what God has gifted them with and to help them learn how to be proud of what God has given them. I encourage you to read Matthew 25:14–30. It's the Parable of the Talents, and I believe it gives a wonderful picture of what God desires for us to do with the *talents* that He's given us.

With social media, accolades, and the constant drive to boast about what we have (more on that to come), it is a very strong temptation to be envious of others. God didn't make a mistake, and He didn't leave you unequipped for your purpose. Believe that everything you need, you have and then be proactive in making sure your players understand that same thing on your team.

Let these verses encourage you, as you pursue a program of appreciation.

> For where jealousy and selfish ambition exist,
> there will be disorder and every vile practice.
> (James 3:16)

You desire and do not have, so you murder. You covet and cannot obtain, so you fight and quarrel. You do not have, because you do not ask. You ask and do not receive, because you ask wrongly, to spend it on your passions. (James 4:2–3)

A tranquil heart gives life to the flesh, but envy makes the bones rot. (Proverbs 14:30)

Fret not yourself because of evildoers, and be not envious of the wicked, for the evil man has no future; the lamp of the wicked will be put out. (Proverbs 24:19–20)

For jealously makes a man furious, and he will not spare when he takes revenge. (Proverbs 6:34)

Keep your life free from love of money, and be content with what you have, for he said, "I will never leave you nor forsake you." (Hebrews 13:5)

Chapter 6

It Does Not Boast, It Is Not Proud

Arrogance—a word that very few people can be labeled without immediately becoming defensive. And the people who don't care if others perceive them as arrogant typically aren't liked by a lot of people. It's interesting to me that arrogance is such an easy thing to fall into, but at the same time, we don't like that quality about people. It's a quality that has the potential to taint everything about a person and make them difficult to be around. This chapter is going to cover both boastfulness and pridefulness and how they are similar yet different. I want to address them separately because of the issues that they cause individually. From what I've experienced in the area of arrogance, I think that boastfulness deals more with what comes out of someone's mouth. Pridefulness deals more with a person's heart, mind-set, and how they carry themselves. Someone who struggles with boastfulness has a problem keeping a reign over their tongue. The issue of pride is an internal conflict that can show up in boasting, but it also has the potential to be exhibited in others ways.

It Does Not Boast

Bragging is something that most people distain, because it's so easy to recognize in a person. I would be willing to bet that some of you had a specific person in mind when you got to this chapter and you said to yourself, "I need to let _____ read *this* chapter!"

It's such an ugly trait because it pushes people away and makes the accused very difficult to be around or talk to. People are made for community and relationships, so when something that we do pushes people away from us, it can be very damaging if we don't recognize it and get it under control.

Boastfulness is a by-product of a person having pride in their heart. Matthew 12:34 says, "For out of the abundance of the heart the mouth speaks." When a person's heart gets filled up with anything in life, it is going to spill out of their mouth. That's how you can tell what is in a person's heart—just listen to what they talk about regularly. The mouth is the ventilation system for the heart. So if you were thinking of a specific person when you got to this chapter or if you are that person, it's important to understand that the solution to boastfulness isn't as simple as getting the person to keep their mouth shut. That would be the same as thinking you could stop an apple tree from producing its fruit by plucking a few off the branch. It's the roots that must dealt with.

Notice Matthew used the word abundance, and some translations use the word overflow. When someone struggles with bragging, it's not because they have a small issue with thinking too highly of themselves. In fact, the person has such a large root of pride within them that it is actually seeping out of them. That's why I believe it's vital that we love people in our lives that find every opportunity to brag about themselves. There is a root that needs to be cut down, and love can begin to do that.

At the beginning of the book, we talked about emotional needs and how children who don't get a particular need met as a child will develop destructive habits in adulthood to fulfill them. A key emotional need that is tied to boastfulness is approval. When a person doesn't receive approval during their adolescence, it's very common for them to have an issue with boastfulness in adulthood. Everyone wants to know that they have the approval of their parents. It's a key element in validating a child's worth. So when a person doesn't experience that in childhood, they are going to seek it out through other means when they're older. Sports are a great replacement for this emotional need because when we do something well, we typically receive applause. And applause to a person who has a deficiency of approval is like giving cocaine to an addict. It will make them feel good for a period of time, but it will always make them crave more.

Some people might brag because they are anxious about what other people's opinion of them are, so they search for ways to make the people around them have reason to think highly of them. The sad thing about this method is it typically makes the exact opposite reaction happen in relationships. Other people might brag because they are self-absorbed and think about themselves far too much. When they are in conversations with other people, they are constantly thinking about themselves, so everything they have to say is usually centered on them. Whatever the motive or intent behind boastfulness is, it can ruin relationships in life, and it can destroy team chemistry in sports.

Here's something very sobering to consider. Everything that we have in life is in no way a result of us being solely responsible for it. Anything that you can find reason to brag about is something you didn't acquire by yourself. If you are very attractive and people affirm that either in person or on social media, your parents are responsible for what you look like. If you have an expensive wardrobe, tons of shoes, or high-end jewelry, either you were born into a family that had the wealth to afford that stuff or you were offered a job by someone that afforded you the income to buy those things. And if the latter is true, you were able to get that job because of the gifts and talents that God gave you. If you are extremely intelligent or very skilled in a certain area, you may have developed that gift over the course of your life, but other people gave you opportunities to develop your gift, and God gave you the raw ability when you were born. You can go down the list of everything imaginable that people boast about in life, and there will always be one common denominator—nobody can take full credit for anything. Everything is a by-product of opportunities, abilities, and gifts given to you by someone else.

Now this shouldn't discourage anyone or give you a reason to feel worthless. It's for the purpose of keeping everything in our lives in perspective. If we are able to daily remind ourselves of this, it will help us maintain an attitude of gratitude for things we could easily boast about. When we live a life of thankfulness for the things that we have, it actually draws people toward us.

It Is Not Proud

I stood in the living room of my grandparent's house in Belle Plaine, Iowa, as a soon-to-be seventh grader who wasn't afraid of anything. Arrogance was no stranger to me, and I welcomed any opportunity that presented a chance for me to impress somebody. On this particular summer day, there was a dilemma, as we had reason to believe there was a bat that got into the house. It had swooped through the living room once or twice, which had everyone on edge knowing it was loose in the house. This was the only topic of conversation that afternoon as the jokes, fears, and strategies of how to capture the bat drowned out the sound of Bob Barker announcing who made it to the final show case on *the Price Is Right* in the background.

I had never seen a bat in real life, and to my knowledge, they weren't much different than birds. I actually wasn't even sure how people could tell the difference between the two just by seeing them fly by. Don't get me wrong, seeing them up close and personal while pausing on the Discovery Channel for a few minutes wasn't the most enjoyable experience, but I certainly didn't have reason to be afraid of them. As my mom was talking with my grandma about ways they could trap the intruder, my brother and I sat on the living room floor joking about the many outcomes this situation could have.

As the possibility of catching the bat with our bare hands was brought up, my grandmother quickly used the opportunity to tell us how dangerous that was because of the potential of getting bit, contracting rabies, and probably some other terrifying, yet unlikely, outcomes. Due to my arrogance and creative imagination, I stood up from the living room rug and began to describe how easy it would be to knock the bat out of midair with a baseball bat. After all, Ken Griffey Jr. was my all-time favorite baseball player, so I knew how to handle the "high heat."

My mom had just come back into the living room and sat down on the sofa as I pantomimed a heroic story of the bat flying through the room only to meet the barrel of my Louisville Slugger in a head-on collision. Doing my best impression of my childhood hero Ken Griffey Jr., I acted as if I was turning my hat around backward, as he did for the home run derby, and stared through the door leading to the hallway as if trying to intimidate John Smoltz on the mound. I got comfortable in my batting stance and acted like I was awaiting the pitch, when things turned for the worst. I said, "I hope that bat comes in here. I'll show it who's boss." And then I said three infamous words that will never be forgotten in the McBeth household. In finishing the charade, I got ready to swing my imaginary bat and said, "Come to papa!" No sooner than the words left my mouth did that bat come soaring through the living room. It streaked right above my head and out the doorway on the other side of the room as I leaped into my mom's lap, screaming in absolute terror.

I have no idea to this day if she was hurt when I crashed into her, because she was laughing hysterically. After the shock of being startled went away, my fear quickly turned into embarrassment. I was mortified thinking how tough I acted and wanted my family to think I was, and I ended up looking more scared than anyone. Luckily, my family was gracious, and it has now turned into a story that we will share for years to come, but I learned a very valuable lesson that day. I had never known the Bible to be so literal before that moment, and while that story is incredibly funny, I wanted to use it to bring up a truth of God's Word—"Pride goes before destruction, and haughtiness before a fall" (Proverbs 16:18).

Sports are infused with pride. It makes sense, because sports are a constant measuring stick of one's ability to be better at a particular skill than someone else. It's also natural for us to want others to acknowledge our success—not only acknowledge it but also be impressed. The root of this desire goes back to one of the emotional needs that each person needs during their upbringing, acceptance. Young men and women who grow up not receiving a *healthy* dose of acceptance are going to be deficient in that area as an adult, and consequently they are going to seek out opportunities to fill that need in their lives. Why do we see so much pridefulness in athletes today? I believe in some people it goes back to individuals either having parents who praised their kids too much and didn't teach them the value of humility or having parents who didn't affirm them enough and now as grown-ups, they don't handle compliments or praise appropriately.

It's important to understand that pridefulness isn't all bad; it is simply an abuse of good self-esteem. Being prideful means to have an excessively high opinion of oneself. Like most things in life, anything that is done in excess can become a problem. So the question then becomes, how do we find a good balance of self-confidence without allowing it to become pridefulness, and where are these issues showing up in sports that we can address and correct?

Confidence is one of the most valuable components to success not only in sports but also in life. Having a belief that you can accomplish whatever task is put in front of you makes the difference between a good athlete and a great one, a successful businessman and an average one. The Bible even confirms this, "For as a man thinketh in his heart, so is he" (Proverbs 23:7, KJV). What we believe in our mind happens in time. I find it amazing that God's Word tells us the thoughts we think have the ability to shape who we are. Our minds are that powerful! That is why professional athletes have started spending thousands, if not millions, of dollars to meet with sports psychologists and get their thoughts under control. They clearly don't have a lack of talent, but to perform night in and night out at the highest level, they know they have to think right.

There is a fine line between confidence and cockiness, and I believe it's a hard line to find. Where is the sweet spot between believing you can accomplish whatever you set your mind on and not letting your ego get too big? And how do you teach and model for your players what it looks like to live humbly yet have the utmost confidence in yourself? I believe it comes down to knowing your place and your purpose.

I know the story about me and the bat was funny, but I actually struggled with arrogance for the majority of my life and would say I still have to keep an eye out for it. There has always been a desire in me to make sure people know who I am and how good I am. The way I walked, how I drew people's attention to myself, and how my heart would light up when I did something impressive in front of a group of people is something I have battled for most of my life. People in the sports world would probably argue that you have to have a cocky edge to yourself to really be good, but I don't think you can find that anywhere in scripture. Jesus was our living example of how to live as Christians and he was the antithesis of cocky. "And being found in appearance of man, He humbled Himself and became obedient to death—even death on a cross!" (Philippians 2:8, NIV).

This urge inside of me to want people to notice me was not godly. It was selfish. Many of my friends in high school and college would tell me that I was arrogant, and that word would pierce right through my puffed-up chest deep into the innermost parts of my soul. In my defensiveness, I tried to argue with them how I wasn't cocky, but deep down, I knew they were recognizing a flaw in my character that I really didn't like. Why was I like this? Why couldn't I shut it off? And how was I ever going to detach my mind from these prideful motives of mine?

"Humble yourselves, therefore, under God's mighty hand, that he may lift you up in due time. Cast all your anxiety on him because he cares for you" (1 Peter 5:6–7).

I had heard these two verses separately since I was a kid, and for whatever reason, I never realized that the two verses went side by side and supported each other. I understood that God calls us to be humble because He is the One who ultimately promotes us and shows us favor. I also understood that whenever we are anxious about something, God wants us to bring those things to Him. God wants you to run to Him with your burdens, your worries, and your doubts because He truly cares for you. What I didn't know until later in life is how putting those two verses together would be the key to setting me free.

How does humility and anxiousness go together? For me, it came down to who I truly thought was in control of my life. While I knew that Jesus was my Savior and God wanted me to give Him lordship in my life, I was much more comfortable letting Him ride shotgun. I knew my eternity was sealed in heaven, but I wanted to call the shots down here on earth. That broken way of thinking made me believe that I was responsible for what I achieved in life. If I wanted to attract a female to be in relationship with, I had to make sure they all noticed me and how dope I was. If I wanted to have a lot of friends and be popular, I had to make sure they knew how fun I was to be around. If I wanted a college scholarship, I had to make sure my arm sleeve, swagger, and subtle celebrations would attract every eye in the gym to how talented I was. Everything was on my shoulders to make it far in life. And while I have never dealt with anxiety, it was stressful to feel the need to always get people to notice me.

As my relationship grew deeper with God, I started to change my thinking about what being a Christ-follower actually looked like. I began to understand that my gifts and talents had been leased to me in *expectation* that I would be a good steward of them. They were never mine, and I would be responsible for how I chose to use them during my short time on this earth. This truth started changing me from the inside out. It was no longer me trying to force myself not to walk into a room with the arrogant swag I used to; it was about transforming my mind daily to realize how thankful I was to even have the gifts I was borrowing. At that point, it became easier to want to use those talents to give thanks to the One who entrusted me with them, and as I humbled myself, God began to promote me.

This brings us back to knowing our place and our purpose. Everyone has been given a measure of talents, and everyone has been given a sphere of influence that they get to impact with their life. Knowing your place is understanding that you have been put on assignment to be the best version of yourself, in the place that you're in, as long as you're there. Too often we become prideful because we think we're "too good" for the position that we currently hold. We think if God would just let us get that promotion or help us get into that school or find our spouse, *then* our full potential could be reached. That is pride. That is us thinking that we are the center of our own universe and that God needs to work around our schedule. But if you go back and read what the end of verse says, it says that

He will lift you up *in due time*. This is what we have such a hard time getting on board with. We want to determine when our time for promotion is due, but that's not up to us to decide.

Understanding our purpose is probably of greater importance. This is what really helped me be released from the clutches of my own arrogance. Our purpose in the time we've been given on this earth is twofold. The first, and most important, is to be in an authentic, passionate relationship with God in heaven and live according to his standards of conduct. The second is of equal importance, and that is to glorify Him and make His Name great by the way that we live and teach others to follow his standards. When this becomes your purpose, you view life through a lens that doesn't allow much room for pridefulness. When you're not busy being humbled by how much you don't deserve God's unfailing love, you're trying to live in a way that draws the attention off you and on to the One who truly deserves it.

What does this look like in sports? Obviously, the goal is to win. To do that, we have to work incredibly hard to perfect the skills of our game. Then we must step into the arena of competition and perform those skills at our highest level to achieve the prize. The problem in sports is when we are successful at anything, our sinful nature wants to brag about it. It wants to shine a light on how incredible we are and let people praise us for it. Then when you add a room full of people who are impressed by the talent that we have and cheer for our accomplishments, it fuels the fire of our ego. The longer this continues without recognizing that we were never designed to store up that praise, roots of pride begin to grow in our hearts that become difficult to dig up.

Go to a collegiate sporting event, or a professional one, and see how the players respond to the crowds. The applause erupts, and you can almost see the player's head grow twice its size as they want all eyes to remain on them. Watch a player during a road game make an incredible play, and as the fans begin to boo, it sparks something inside of them that turns their mind-set into an "all of you against me" type mentality. Please know that I love competition, and I am all for players enjoying the game, but the most important thing is that we remember not to fall in love with the praises of other people, unless it's about the team and not just about you. Having a "we not me" attitude will prevent self-confidence from turning into selfishness.

This is what I want coaches to teach their players. The game of basketball is a wonderful game filled with excitement, anxiousness, joy, and sorrow. There's absolutely a place for celebrating, having fun, and enjoying the success that you work so hard to achieve; but when it's not managed properly, it is a slippery slope to a place of arrogance. Regardless of what level of basketball you coach, it's important to pay attention to how your team handles success. The most threatening part of pride in my opinion is that it separates an individual from the rest of the team. When a player starts to become too consumed with his stats, accolades, or praise, they begin to think it's more about themselves than it is about the team. This is something that needs to be monitored regularly in your program.

As a coach, you need to remember that pride doesn't show up after one moment of selfishness. It develops over time when a player's ego isn't managed correctly. It would be wise to look for these tendencies when you're recruiting players and let potential prospects know early on that nobody will ever be bigger than the team in your program. For coaches that have tryouts, I would watch very closely for prideful motives when you decide who you're going to give roster spots to. And for coaches that don't have the option of recruiting and your players are given to you, this is something you should get a feel for early in your season and begin to take care of any issues as soon as possible.

Pride is always a potential threat whether you're on a successful team or a bad one. There are so many voices that your players hear from on a daily basis, and it's impossible to silence all of them. That's why, as a coach, you need to have regular conversations that keep everyone focused on the same goal. The last thing I would recommend is to be intentional about making sure the stars of your team are serving the rest of the players in your program. The threat of pride is always greater for your best players, and that threat is always trying to pull them away from the unity of team. By intentionally finding small ways to make sure the best players are serving the rest of the team, it reminds everyone in the program that no one is inherently more important than anyone else, regardless of what someone's scoring average is.

The hard truth that people don't hear enough is that this life is not about us. We are incredibly small pieces in a much bigger picture. To accept this reality is not demeaning of yourself or your worth, but it is putting life into proper perspective. Human beings have decided that we enjoy entertainment, and basketball happens to be one of the things that we are entertained by. Basketball players and coaches are no more important than any other group of people in other fields. Our gift just so happens to entertain people. Our purpose doesn't become more valuable simply because of the gifts that we've been given to manage. If anything, our responsibility to be humble becomes greater because of the temptation of pride that comes with sports. Jesus Christ wasn't just our Savior, but He was God made flesh. He was in a position to be more arrogant, and with good reason, than anyone who's ever walked the face of the earth. But He chose to be a living example of humility. His mission was to advance the kingdom of His Father by serving, rather than being served. No matter how talented we are, we don't measure up to a fraction of the glory of the Son of God. When we are tempted to boast about who we are or what we've accomplished, let us be reminded of the example Christ set for us.

> This is what the LORD says: "Let not the wise boast of their wisdom or the strong boast of their strength or the rich boast of their riches, but let the one who boasts boast about this: that they have the understanding to know me, that I am the LORD, who exercises kindness, justice and righteousness on earth, for in these I delight," declares the LORD. (Jeremiah 9:23–24)

> The LORD detests all the proud of heart. Be sure of this: They will not go unpunished. (Proverbs 16:5)

Haughty eyes, a proud heart, and evil actions are all sin. (Proverbs 21:4)

Humble yourselves before the Lord, and he will lift you up. (James 4:10)

When pride comes, then comes disgrace, but with humility comes wisdom. (Proverbs 11:2)

For by the grace given me I say to every one of you: Do not think of yourself more highly than you ought, but rather think of yourself with sober judgment, in accordance with the faith God has distributed to each of you. (Romans 12:3)

For you know the grace of our Lord Jesus Christ, that though he was rich, yet for your sake he became poor, so that you through his poverty might become rich. (2 Corinthians 8:9)

Chapter 7

It Does Not Dishonor Others

America celebrates dishonor. Whether it's the main theme in the household of a Netflix original or slander that gets retweeted on Twitter, we don't hesitate to disrespect people. Our country as a whole is more disrespectful to authority than any time in the history of our nation. Regardless of whether you affiliate with the Republican or Democratic Party, listen to the things that are said about our president. If we don't feel an obligation to show honor to the leader of our country, then who is deserving of honor? It is remarkable how little value we place on honor. I preface this next statement by saying that I recognize there are police officers who make bad decisions, have racial prejudices, and have issues of their own; but the way that we view and talk about our law enforcement is appalling. And I believe that this is a trait that is trending downward through the generations. When I speak to people of Generation X (forty to fifty-nine) and especially the baby boomers (fifty-nine to seventy-three), it's something I hear mentioned a lot—the lack of respect for authority.

Other translations of 1 Corinthians 13 say, "It does not behave rudely." If we look at ourselves in today's culture, I believe this is another area that we are becoming more corrupt in. The way children speak to teachers, and the way kids talk to their parents, is consistent with how coaches put down their players, and players do the same to their teammates. We spoke about this issue when we addressed kindness, but I want to reiterate the plague that is consuming our daily conversations and relationships. Notice it doesn't say, "It does not speak rudely." Our actions have the ability to be just as rude as our words. Quite often, our body language speaks much louder than what comes out of our mouths. To love one another, we must get control over the rude things we say and the way we behave rudely toward the people around us. It is amazing what happens when people show simple acts of kindness, because it is unfortunately becoming such a rare commodity in our society.

One of my favorite people to listen to is Ron Carpenter. He is a pastor/apostle that is the head of Redemption Church in the Bay Area, California, and spent a large portion of his ministry in Greenville, South Carolina. He is one of the most anointed people I've ever heard pick up a microphone, and he speaks a lot about honor. One of the things I've heard him say is that honor needs to be our standard, regardless of whether the recipient is honorable or not. This concept is backward from how the majority of people think. It's common to have the mind-set that we will show someone honor if, and when, the person gives us reason to honor them. But *agape* doesn't look like that. Love holds every person in high regard independent of who the person is or what the person acts like.

Honor is a trait that is learned through recognition and practice, which means as coaches we have the responsibility of developing honor in our players. Because of the issue of broken homes, which we previously discussed, I think one of the balls that gets dropped in a child's upbringing is learning the value and importance of honor. This means that coaches may be fighting an uphill battle with incoming players based on what their homelife was like. It becomes that much more important that coaches are dedicated to not only teaching but also showing honor to combat bad habits their players might bring with them.

There is only one commandment out of the Ten that God gave Moses that had a promise attached to it—"Honor your father and your mother, so that you may live long in the land the Lord your God is giving you" (Exodus 20:12, NIV). The first thing to address about this verse is how problematic it becomes when there is not a father and mother in the house for the child to honor. Secondly, the verse gives a promise that a child's ability to show honor is actually attached to their life span! God doesn't play around when it comes to honor.

Why is honor so valuable to God that He would attach longevity of life to it and make it one of the cornerstones of love? Because honor is the key to access. This is another principle that I learned from Ron Carpenter. Every person was created with a certain measure of gifts/talents. They were given to each of us so they could bless others and give glory back to God. This means that God set up the world in a way that each person is walking around on a daily basis with gifts that were meant for others to benefit from. One person has a singing voice that sounds almost angelic, and it blesses those who hear them. One person has the ability to create amazing things with their hands for other people's use. One person is able to teach in such a profound way that they can explain the most difficult concepts to anyone. Another person is a natural-born leader who is able to organize people to achieve a goal. The common thread in every gift is that they are meant to benefit others. That is why pride is so destructive. When a person becomes self-absorbed, they are deceived into believing their gift is for their own benefit, and they abuse the gift.

Honor is so important, because honor grants access to a person's gift. Mark 6 shows us an example of this. If you read the four gospels (Matthew, Mark, Luke, and John), you will see that Jesus was going from city to city cleaning out hospitals and healing all who were sick or afflicted. The word spread about the miracles that Jesus was doing, and every place He showed up at, people brought their sick to Him expecting that He could heal them. After Jesus's ministry had taken off, He returned to his hometown, and this is where we pick up the story.

> Jesus left there and went to his hometown, accompanied by his disciples. When the Sabbath came, he began to teach in the synagogue, and many who heard him were amazed. "Where did this man get these things?" they asked. "What's

> this wisdom that has been given him? What
> are these remarkable miracles he is performing?
> Isn't this the carpenter? Isn't this Mary's son and
> the brother of James, Joseph, Judas and Simon?
> Aren't his sisters here with us?" And they took
> offense at him. Jesus said to them, "A prophet
> is not without honor except in his own town,
> among his relatives and in his own home." He
> could not do any miracles there, except lay his
> hands on a few sick people and heal them. He
> was amazed at their lack of faith. (Mark 6:1–6)

The Son of man was on a mission to preach the gospel, set the captives free, and heal all who were sick and afflicted when He came back to his hometown, and something very strange happened. In verse 5, it said, "He could not do any miracles there, except lay his hands on a few sick people and heal them." This doesn't make sense. Jesus had been traveling around Israel not just curing a few headaches, but Matthew 4:23 says, "Jesus went throughout Galilee, teaching in their synagogues, proclaiming the good news of the kingdom, and healing every disease and sickness among the people." How then could He arrive in His hometown, where all of His childhood friends and family were, and His gift seem to lose its power? When I picture Jesus returning to the place He grew up, after having done the incredible miracles He was doing, I imagine the people welcoming Him the way the Bay Area celebrated the Golden State Warriors when they returned from Cleveland with the coveted NBA Finals Championship trophy—droves of people lining the streets, as the echoes from the cheers could be heard across the Golden Gate Bridge. But sadly, his not-so warm welcoming was more closely related to the boos LeBron James received during his return to Quicken Loans Arena as he was introduced on the Miami Heat starting lineup.

Instead of people honoring the Savior of the world as He returned to bring His gift to His friends and family, He was met with rude comments questioning how "the mere carpenter" could possibly do such miraculous things. The people were offended by Him.

And because of the offense they took, the Bible says He could do no mighty work there. Jesus's gift, given to Him by His Father, that He eagerly wanted to bless His hometown with, was rendered ineffective, not because of something He did, but because of the lack of honor shown to Him by people who were unfortunately too familiar with His background to accept such a marvelous gift.

We need to learn a valuable lesson from the people of Nazareth about the importance of honor. The lesson is what we honor moves toward us and what we dishonor moves away from us. I can say confidently that there were people in Nazareth that day who needed healing that didn't receive it. But we don't receive the gift on other people's lives because of need; we access it when we honor them. I can almost see the disappointment on Jesus's face, as He looked at His friends and relatives, knowing that they were going to miss out on something so powerful.

We have the opportunity in sports to honor a lot of different people as coaches and players—administrators, fans, referees, janitors, former players/alumni, the community, the media, other teams at your school, your opponent, and many others—not to mention how important it is for players and coaches to honor one another. The problem that I find in sports today is that we have a way of only showing honor to people that we believe are important. We'll go out of our way to shake hands with the donor who gives a bunch of money to our program, but we will just as quickly avoid a long conversation with the team bus driver, because they can't do as much for us. It's a harsh reality, but it's the truth.

We talked about how honor is the key to access, and we cannot get the gift from a person without honoring them first. I think that can come across as a selfish principle that we should treat people well so we can get something from them in return. I believe God's desire is much deeper than that. When we honor someone, we give the person dignity and self-worth, and the best version of that person comes out. And *that* should be our ultimate goal—to see people be the best version of themselves.

Among your team, I believe you need to place a high priority on players and coaches honoring one another, from the star to the guy who never players, and that players honor every coach regardless of whether they are the head coach or a volunteer. It's also important that every manager or student assistant is treated with the same honor. What does this look like practically? In a team where every person makes honor a priority, each individual on the team feels that they matter and have worth, no matter what role they hold. Managers don't get talked down to because they're not important. Star players don't think it's the job of a bench warmer to rebound for them, simply because they are a better player. Players don't think they can talk back to or disrespect an assistant coach just because the head coach isn't around. Coaches don't belittle their players because of their place of authority.

If anyone in your program feels that they don't have much worth or don't feel valued, my guess is that they haven't been shown enough honor by the people in the program. As a coach, this is your responsibility to fix—because just like a team that plays their best basketball when all five guys on the court are working together and playing with confidence, a team built on a foundation of honor gets the best out of each person in the program. If you are a coach reading this book, I challenge you to have an intentional conversation with each player on your team and ask them if they feel honored and respected on the team. I think the feedback you get will surprise you!

I've seen this issue with a lot of teams. Coaches need to lead the way by showing honor to their players, and I think this is something coaches struggle to achieve. I know that coaches generally like their players and want to see them succeed, but I think that a lot of coaches have gone away from honoring them. There is an unspoken dynamic on teams today where the coach is more of a master and the players are viewed more as slaves rather than coaches being teachers and instructors.

Honor means to hold someone in high respect or great esteem. It's not like a salary, where it's given out in different amounts depending on the person or job title. It is a standard set by the giver no matter who the recipient is. This means that if you, as a coach, don't scream at your own kids when they make a mistake, then you shouldn't scream at your players for making one. If you wouldn't tell your boss that "he sucks" and is "terrible at his job," then it's not appropriate to say that to your players. If you would punish your star player for missing class by making him run five suicides, but you'd make the kid who never plays run fifteen to "make an example out of him" because you don't care if he pukes since he can't help you win, then that's a lack of honor. Whatever standard of honor you've set for one person in your program, you should give to everyone else.

That doesn't mean that each person on your team is going to get the same amount of playing time or responsibility; it just means that they're all held in high respect by you. As coaches, we need to go out of our way to do everything with honor and respect toward our players. How you treat them will make a large impact on how they view themselves long after they're no longer your player.

An area that I struggle with that I have been working on is showing honor to the people that I come in contact with on a daily basis that aren't on our team. I get into a habit of being so consumed with what I have to do for the day that I can be short with people or not give them the attention or respect they deserve. One specific area that I catch myself doing this is with the janitor at our school. He is one of the hardest-working, diligent people at our university, and to this day, I don't know that I've ever seen him with anything but a smile on his face. I don't treat him poorly or disrespect him, but I notice that on the occasion when he comes into my office and wants to talk, I tend to be more focused on my work than on him wanting to engage with me. It goes back to what I just said about how you treat each of your players. If the athletic director walked into my office to talk with me, my computer would get closed, my phone would be turned to silent, and he would have my full attention. I know in my life God is calling me to *agape* in this area of my life.

One last thing I would like to address is the issue of familiarity. If you go back to the story in Mark 6, it was the people who had known Jesus the longest that were offended by Him. And Jesus recognized this when He said, "A prophet is not without honor except in his own town, among his relatives and in his own home." We tend to become so familiar with the people closest to us that we get comfortable and lose our honor for them. Children do this with their parents when they enter into adulthood. We see this in marriages when a husband who used to be in awe of his bride as she walked into the room begin to not notice when she gets her hair done. It happens in the workplace when an employee stops calling his boss Ms. Anderson and starts referring to her by Karen. This also happens on teams between players and coaches over time. We must not allow our level of honor to be diminished as we further our relationships with people. It's important that we recognize that this is a natural tendency and we must be on the lookout for people in our lives whom we have lost honor for and reestablish that relationship.

Because God's Word is so consistent about His standard of honor, I believe it's important that we examine our relationships and determine if we are honoring people appropriately. Our nation has been poisoned with the acceptance of disrespect. On our teams and in our daily relationships, let's raise our standard of honor so we can love people differently!

> So in everything, do to others what you would have them do to you, for this sums up the Law and the Prophets. (Matthew 12:7, NIV)

> Love must be sincere. Hate what is evil; cling to what is good. Be devoted to one another in love. Honor one another above yourselves. (Romans 12:9–10, NIV)

> Show proper respect to everyone, love the family of believers, fear God, honor the emperor. (1 Peter 2:17, NIV)

> Now we ask you, brothers and sisters, to acknowledge those who work hard among you, who care for you in the Lord and who admonish you. Hold them in the highest regard in love because of their work. Live in peace with each other. (1 Thessalonians 5:12–13, NIV)

Do nothing out of selfish ambition or vain conceit. Rather, in humility value others above yourselves, not looking to your own interests but each of you to the interests of the others. (Philippians 2:3–4, NIV)

Chapter 8

It Is Not Self-seeking

Being a great athlete demands investing a lot of time on yourself. To tell you that a person is able to fully commit to their particular sport and not have any self-centeredness would simply be untrue. Like most skills in life, sports require that you invest a lot into your development. What we need to discover in *The Sweet Sixteen* is how we can be involved in a game that requires us to focus on ourselves, but not make <u>life</u> about us.

Selfishness is not something that we have to be taught. We come into this world already being selfish creatures. That's why one of the first words that infants learn to say in context is "mine"—and boy do they fall in love with it quickly! Our human nature is designed to take care of ourselves first and worry about everything else later. This means that we must first come to grips with the reality that self-seeking is a part of our makeup, and we are going to have to fight our selfish desires daily if we want to overcome it. This is not a one-hitter-quitter knockout fight. It's an ongoing battle that tries to seep into every season of your life.

To be a great athlete, you must spend large amounts of time on yourself. Between academics, practice, weight training, skill development, nutrition, film study, and more, the demand on an athlete's time is at a premium. When I was in college, I rarely had time during my week that was free from scheduled activities, and when I did, I wanted to spend it doing what I wanted. The reason why athletics digs such deep roots of self-centeredness is because of the competitiveness and accolades that are attached to sports. How many successful athletes can you think of that would say they are "completely content" with their current amount of success? Very few! Because no matter how impressive a person's athletic resume gets, there will always be another milestone in front of them, begging to be chased. Our culture's priority falls right in line with rapper DJ Khaled who said, "All I do is win, win, win no matter what."

Winning produces one of the most euphoric experiences known to man. It's borderline intoxicating. It's one of the very few things in life that can make a group of grown men jump around together like they were back in elementary school. The climactic buildup to the final buzzer that produces an outburst of joy is unmatched by most thrills in life. Winning is the motivation that drives people to train countless hours just to experience those few moments of ecstasy. The issue starts when the sweet taste of victory becomes so overwhelming that the means in which we travel to achieve it become destructive. When victory becomes more than a goal and turns into our heart's desire, it changes us as people. It makes life become a game board for us to navigate through, searching for every possible checkpoint to crown us winners at the finish line. We become self-absorbed, and blinders are fastened around our eyes to anything that's not going to help us win.

This internal motivation to win is a good quality, don't get me wrong. God created humans with the internal drive to push through obstacles to achieve success. It's in our nature. But like most things, the key to living a life filled with purpose and joy is to keep things in balance. I had a teacher growing up who had a powerful phrase that I think of quite often. He would frequently say that "the main thing is to keep the main thing, the main thing." God is the Creator, Orchestrator, and Sustainer of everything in this world. He is the main thing. When we align all of our wants and desires up according to His Word, which calls us to humble ourselves and put others first, He will give us the desires of our heart (Matthew 6:33).

*****

One area of basketball that I think we mishandle is *change*. Change happens in life as we grow up, but it also happens in basketball. And in both life and basketball, if we don't adjust to change, we can find ourselves very frustrated. Genesis 8:22 says, "While the earth remains, seedtime and harvest, cold and heat, winter and summer, and day and night shall not cease." No matter what happens in this world, here's something that you can be certain of—things will continue to change. *Nothing* stays the same! It's important that we understand that, because it will help us deal with the highs and lows of life. So if change is inevitable, then we need to expect it and be willing to change with it.

The majority of coaches were former players. And in many cases, the coach was a very good player. And to be a good player, it typically requires all the commitments that we talked at the beginning of the chapter. This means a large percentage of coaches at one point in their life dedicated most of their time to this game of basketball so *they* could be successful. What can be a stumbling block for a lot of coaches is the change that is *required* when going from a player to a coach. What is demanded of your position is quite different, and I see a lot of coaches struggle in this transition.

As a player, everything is always about you. "*You* need to get more shots up." "*You* need to lift at least four times a week." "*You* need to get at least a 3.0 GPA." "*You* need to score at least twenty tonight if we're gonna have a chance to win." The focal point of everything you hear on a daily basis is all about your performance. This creates a pattern of understanding that life is about you. That priority #1 is always going to be yourself. But just as we talked about, life never stays the same, and it's imperative that we change as life changes. As a coach, it no longer is about you. Your role as a coach is to make your program about your players. And as easy as this sounds, I believe it is something that a lot of coaches fumble during the transition between their season of life as a player and their new season as a coach.

Coaches are responsible for the well-being of every player on their team, whether it's six golfers or 120 football players. That doesn't leave a lot of time for a coach to be worried about their personal agendas. Far too often, I see coaches who want everything to be about them. They want to be in the spotlight, they want the attention on them, and they want for their name to be in people's mouths as often as possible. I believe this arrogance stems from pride not being addressed and fixed during the coaches' time as a player. Cocky players rarely become humble coaches. And in some cases, it might not even be an issue of arrogance, but of prioritizing your time. As a player, your time was typically about you. As a coach, your time needs to be about your players.

This is why as a coach, it is necessary to be intentional about creating a culture where *We>Me*. Because of our natural tendency to always take care of ourselves and our wants, there has to be a strong culture that celebrates team success and doesn't stand for selfishness. You can make such a profound impact on each of your players by helping them adapt an attitude of selflessness during critical years of their lives. Because if you can get your players to care more about team success than their personal achievements, that will help them know how to put their kids and their spouse first. It will help them think of the well-being of the company they work for rather than their own recognition. It may even help them want to take care of people who have very little, instead of desiring the latest and greatest things in life.

Here are some ways to create a culture of selflessness. Some of these are very practical, and some of them might take time to implement. Regardless of what standards you create, make sure your players understand how/why these standards create the culture that you want. I am a firm believer that the millennial generation is quick to question rules, but when they believe in the purpose of them, they'll follow them with passion.

Points aren't the only stat that matters. There are few things in the game of basketball that can create more selfish desires than scoring. To most people, it defines how good of a player someone is. It's the first question that people ask someone after a game. This is one of the first areas that needs to be addressed on your team. Does scoring matter? Absolutely it does. Do the players who score the most points matter more than the others? Absolutely not. This has to be an area that is talked about on a regular basis with your players. It doesn't matter who scores, as long as it's getting done. And the players on the floor need to be bought into a culture where they don't stress about their scoring average, but they truly find joy in seeing their teammates score. One way you can make this become a focal point in your program is by identifying how different players score the ball the best and recognizing that in front of everyone else. If you have a player who can't dribble to save their life, but they can really shoot it, make sure you take time to affirm that in them and to everyone else. If a post player isn't a good shooter, but knows how to get position and score it really easily around the basket, then draw up plays for that player so they can do what they do best. It's also important that other areas of the game get equal amount of recognition and praise as scoring. If getting buckets is the only thing you ever compliment, your players are only going to want to get buckets.

Your competition is not in your locker room. Too often, players are actually happy when their teammates screw up because it means their opportunity to play, or play more, increases. This is a surefire sign that there's a culture of self-seeking in your program. I understand that every player has a desire to play, and there's nothing wrong with that. It becomes destructive when our personal agendas become so important that players would prefer to see their teammates fail for those agendas to be achieved. You can find out a lot about your team by how they celebrate other teammates' successes and how they comfort one another when failure happens. It's critical that you keep an eye out for players who have "I-centered" tendency on multiple occasions. One thing that I've learned from my time at Truman State is our guys constantly high five one another. I mean, it's almost excessive, but the things I've come to notice during my time here is how much it brings them together. I would encourage you to find ways to get your players to intentionally touch. I know that sounds somewhat corny, but there's so much power in touch. Try starting and ending practice with everyone putting their arms around one another in a circle while the coach addresses the team. Find creative ways for your team to stay connected through encouragement and physical touch.

A team is only as strong as its relationships. If you've ever watched high school sports, more specifically state championship games for high schoolers, you'll typically notice that there's something different about those wins and losses. There is more sadness when a team falls short and more uncontrollable joy when a team is crowned victorious. I believe that it is because of the relationships between the players. Most high school teams are made up of players who have done life with one another for potentially most of their lives. The same person hoisting the trophy in the air at center court was the same person at your fifth, sixth, and seventh birthday party. There's history, friendship, and love that go far beyond the sport you play together. There's something so valuable to learn from this. The relationships off the court are what truly make a team on the court. This is something that college players struggle to achieve, as well as professionals, because they are brought together later in life for the purpose of achieving a goal, not building a friendship. As a coach, you must be very intentional about creating daily opportunities for your players to learn about one another and grow as friends. It's easy to view the teammate in your position as a roadblock to your success when you don't know anything about them. It's much harder when you genuinely know them and have built a connection with them outside of the gym. So, coaches, get your players to put down their cell phones and talk to one another! You'll be amazed at how they start to root for one another when their relationship becomes a friendship.

Watch your mouth. How the players and coaches in your program speak is the best indicator of the culture that is established. The way each person on the team talks about the program should be a learned behavior. As a coach, you need to set the example of how your team communicates to one another and how they talk about the goals of each season. It's almost impossible to encourage and uplift the people around you on a daily basis and still only be focused on yourself. It's hard to serve one another each day and over time only care about yourself. If you can create/sustain a culture where speaking life toward one another is a standard, you will begin to see your player's hearts follow their words. A way that you can implement this is by making it a standard that when someone scores a basket off a pass, they need to thank the passer. It seems simple, but words are powerful! You'll be amazed what happens when the communication among your team is uplifting. But remember, it starts at the top. Your players and assistants need to hear *you* focused on the positive things that are happening for them to buy into that philosophy.

Hopefully some of those ideas can stir up your own creative ways to implement a culture of selflessness into your team. But let me say it again, because it can't be said enough—your actions speak much louder than your words.

*****

Having daily reminders and intentional conversations on the concept of *We>Me* is so valuable, because the threat of self-seeking will always be lurking outside the door of your locker room, as well as your coaches' offices. I equate keeping a culture of selflessness to maintaining your physical strength. It takes intentionality and daily disciplines. If you stop lifting weights for three months, you're going to lose both muscle mass and strength. Simply doing a couple of bicep curls from time to time and occasionally going for a jog isn't going to keep your body from regressing.

If you only mention your standard of selflessness from time to time randomly in conversation, or you have a serious talk with your team about individual egos after they've surfaced, you're already playing from behind. This is an area that needs to be at the forefront of your players' and coaches' minds and a part of everything that you do.

My personal struggle with self-seeking has ebbed and flowed throughout the course of my time in sports. Because of my struggle with arrogance growing up that I spoke about earlier and the transformation that happened through the growing in my relationship with God, I had this area of my life under control early in college. When I got to Iowa State, there was such a high standard that I had to reach to be good enough to play that the battle with self-seeking came back in full force. I struggled with looking at my teammates as the competition, rather than my family. I had moments of hope when a teammate of mine wasn't able to play that stemmed from caring more about myself than the team. When you're on a team and you're not playing, it's next to impossible to avoid moments of disappointment about others getting to play when you're not, but *how* you deal with those struggles show your true colors. This is why it's critical that everyone on your team knows the role they play in the bigger picture so they have a sense of purpose.

As an assistant coach, there are still internal battles with self-seeking. There are days when I want to run practice, because I think there are deficiencies in our team that are only recognized by me. There are games when I think I should be sitting in the head chair during time-outs addressing the players. I've been in staff meetings where the decisions that are being made aren't what I would have chosen. The truth is it doesn't matter what role you play on a team; there will *always* be situations, opportunities, and reasons to be selfish. As a follower of Jesus Christ, it is our responsibility to submit all of our issues to God and ask Him to help us in our weakness—to remind ourselves that *it's not about us*!

One day I hope to be a head coach of a program, where I believe the ultimate test of self-seeking begins. As a head coach, you don't really have a lot of checks and balances because you're the top of the line in your program. The place where you're most vulnerable to self-seeking is when you are in charge of calling the shots day in and day out. It becomes incredibly easy to do things in a way that simply make life easier for you. I want to charge head coaches to resist the urge to be selfish simply because you can get away with it. Set the example, and ask your team to follow in your footsteps.

In the first chapter of Genesis, the phrase "after its own kind" is used multiple times. The writer is explaining how everything from seeds, to cattle, to insects, to fruits all produce after their own kind. What does this have to do with a basketball team not being selfish? It's the understanding that a coach will "produce" what he or she already is. An apple tree is never going to produce potatoes. A field planted with corn is never going to produce wheat when harvest time comes. Likewise, a coach who is conceited and preaches humility will never get a humble team. A coach who demands mental toughness but losses their mind when things don't go according to plan will continually be frustrated with the lack of mental toughness. You don't get what you preach; you get what you are.

Here are some incredible verses that you can use to remind yourself and your team what a life of selflessness looks like.

> Don't love the world's ways. Don't love the world's goods. Love of the world squeezes out love for the Father. Practically everything that goes on in the world—wanting your own way, wanting everything for yourself, wanting to appear important—has nothing to do with the Father. It just isolates you from him. The world and all its wanting, wanting, wanting is on the way out—but whoever does what God wants is set for eternity. (1 John 2:15–17, MSG)

> God will repay each person according to what they have done. To those who by persistence in doing good seek glory, honor and immortality, he will give eternal life. But for those who are self-seeking and who reject the truth and follow evil, there will be wrath and anger. (Romans 2:6–8, NIV)

> Then Jesus went to work on his disciples. "Anyone who intends to come with me has to let me lead. You're not in the driver's seat; I am. Don't run from suffering; embrace it. Follow me and I'll show you how. Self-help is no help at all. Self-sacrifice is the way, my way, to finding yourself, your true self. What kind of deal is it to get everything you want but lose yourself? What could you ever trade your soul for? (Matthew 16:24–26, MSG)

The one who blesses others is abundantly blessed; those who help others are helped. (Proverbs 11:25, MSG)

Chapter 9

It Is Not Easily Angered

What is it about losing that changes a person? Is it our culture? Is it a part of human nature? Is it based on personality? How does the fear of not winning bring out a monster that lay dormant inside our hearts until failure is knocking on our front door? Surely some doctor can prescribe some type of medication to paralyze that part of our emotional response system. Does a psychologist have the ability to help me talk my way to a solution? What about a hypnotist that can put me into a deep sleep and order my subconscious to not feel anger anymore? Any of these questions could have crossed your mind over the course of your life in sports, but I think it points to two consistent things—first, we know that anger is something every person struggles with and, second, we know that being angry isn't something we *want* to do.

Some of you reading this book might have had the opportunity to see me grow up. A select few have had the chance to see me when I am playing video games. As a kid, my mom found out very quickly that video games were a very cheap babysitter. My brother and I were the type of boys who would stay glued to the TV screen until our eyes watered, our hands almost fused to the control, and entire days would go by without us realizing it. We were junkies when it came to playing video games. When we woke up, when we can home from school, on the weekends, and even a couple of minutes on Sunday morning before leaving for church (if we could get downstairs quietly enough), we had a longing to "get on the sticks." Looking back, I don't think it was just the fun of playing a game, but it was the passion to win. It didn't matter if it was NCAA College Football, Tony Hawk Pro Skater, Need for Speed, or a silly billiards game. I wanted to *win*! My heart came alive every time I would achieve a character, unlock a new level, or outscore my opponent. It was addicting, and it was fun.

The problem with this enticing console that kept me coming back for more on a daily basis is that I didn't always win. The majority of the time I did, because I was a beast at mastering games, but when I lost, it was quite the experience to witness. I don't know what was more embarrassing—the screaming at the television, the slamming of my control on anything that I knew wouldn't break it (for fear that my mom wouldn't buy me another one), or the actual anxiety that took over, as I thought about the implications of not winning. The truth is it probably all takes a backseat to the tears that would leak down my face, accompanied with some snot, as I dreaded the impending failure about to take place. I was a hot mess! I would actually yell at a TV screen demanding that something wasn't fair or that I had been cheated by the programmers.

I was usually aware of my surroundings enough to make sure my mom didn't hear my pathetic whimpers, but from time to time, I would lose control and begin to complain within earshot of her, and I would be sent into a downward spiral as the words, "Austin! If you can't play that game without getting upset, then I'll just take it away!" came from a nearby room, which naturally made me even more upset. The only thing that could possibly be worse than losing a video game was the thought of having that video game taken away from me. My hope is that some of you reading this can relate to my experience or at least got a good laugh at my expense.

How could a video game stir up such powerful emotions that I felt incapable of not pleading my case to an electric box? What was wrong with me? And furthermore how could someone who is a Christian have that much pent-up anger inside of them? Was I broken? Was I just a terrible child with a future of therapy and counseling ahead of me? For those of you reading that know me now, you know that's not the case. However, there is something deeper to my struggle that I believe we can crack open and let the truth of God's Word help all of us in the areas that we struggle with anger.

For me, it was losing. For some people, it's getting yelled at by a parent or significant other. For some, it's discussions of politics. For others, it's bad drivers. There may be some who are triggered by people simply being constantly messy. Regardless of what your personal trigger is, everyone has something that stirs up anger in them. And when I say everyone, I mean everyone. Jesus Himself even got angry. Look at Mark 11:15–17(MSG):

> They arrived at Jerusalem. Immediately on entering the Temple Jesus started throwing out everyone who had set up shop there, buying and selling. He kicked over the tables of the bankers and the stalls of the pigeon merchants. He didn't let anyone even carry a basket through the Temple. And then he taught them, quoting this text: My house was designated a house of prayer for the nations; You've turned it into a hangout for thieves.

I think it's fair to say the Jesus was upset. In some ways, it sounds a bit like a reenactment from my days of losing at Mario Cart. But I think what is important to take away from this is that we must understand that there *is* a place in the life of a *Sweet Sixteen* coach to be angry, but we must be able to recognize those moments and handle them appropriately.

Ephesians 4:26–27 (AMP) says, "BE ANGRY [at sin—at immorality, at injustice, at ungodly behavior], YET DO NOT SIN; do not let your anger [cause you shame, nor allow it to] last until the sun goes down. And do not give the devil an opportunity [to lead you into sin by holding a grudge, or nurturing anger, or harboring resentment, or cultivating bitterness]."

God actually gives us permission to be angry, but He also gives us parameters for our anger. If we look at Mark 11 and Ephesians 4,

I think we can see how God is consistent about His stance on anger and how Christ's actions line up with them. I want to point out the following five things we need to remember when it comes to dealing with anger:

1. *Be angry.* There is a time and a place for people to be angry. It is a part of our genetic design that situations and circumstances will provoke waves of passion inside of us. People who do everything to fight anger and suppress it at all costs are actually hindering what God can do through their frustration. We need to know that God says we have permission to be angry. It's productive for us to not be okay with certain things in life, when we handle our anger the right way. Anger, when it's handled appropriately, is what motivates us to stand up for things that we believe in. It's the internal lighter fluid that ignites our soul to act instead of remaining silent, when injustices go unaddressed.

2. *Be angry at the right things.* My story of dealing with anger during my childhood is a prime example of being angry at the wrong things. My rage was a result of being immature and not knowing how to handle failure. It's important that we look at the areas of our lives that are a red button for our angry and investigate whether our anger is appropriate. Ephesians 4 says to be angry at immortality, injustice, and ungodly behavior. When Jesus acted out of anger in the temple in Mark 4, the Bible says He did it because God's house was being used inappropriately. He was driven to action by the immoral and ungodly things He saw taking place in His Father's house. We must be honest with ourselves about why certain things make us angry and align them with God's Word. I truly believe that as we allow His Word to transform our thinking, then we will begin to hate what is evil and cling to what is good. God promotes that type of anger, because it shows the world how passionate we are about our Lord and Savior.

3. *Yet do not sin.* I think this is the step that we fail the most at. The Word says that in our anger, we are still called to avoid sinning out of that anger. I think what makes this such a gray area is not only knowing how to act out of anger but also knowing where the line is. Jesus didn't just scold the vendors in the temple, but He tossed over their tables! When I read this, I envision an extremely upset person who wasn't playing any games with these people. But this wasn't considered sin. Clearly your actions are allowed to be passionate and bold and still be appropriate when they are in the right motive. The problem that I struggle with is I like to use Jesus's moment of passion to justify me being upset and lashing out about something that doesn't align with number two.

The word in the Hebrew and Greek for sin was translated to mean two major concepts. The first was an act of transgression, which means "to step across" or "to go beyond a set of boundaries or limits." The second was "to miss the mark" (www.ucg.org). Sin has to do with not staying inside of the boundaries that God has put in place for us or attempting to be compliant with His rules and falling short in our efforts. This is why I believe it's essential that as coaches, parents, and leaders, we have rules and guidelines for the people we are in authority over. People *need* to learn how to stay within certain boundaries and know there are consequences for falling short of expectations. Without it, we will never understand that reality in God's structure. Lastly, it's imperative that we know what God's Word says. If we don't know the boundaries we are supposed to stay within, we are guaranteed to break them. If we don't know what the target is, we are sure to miss it.

4. *Don't let the sun go down on your anger.* This is an area that marriage has really tested me in. Don't go to sleep angry? That makes me angry just thinking about it! It is so incredibly difficult to hit this target that God has put in front of us. My wife and I have a great relationship, and thanks be to God, we rarely have big issues in our relationship. It's mostly little stuff here and there that better commu-

nication could have solved before it became something worth getting angry over, but nevertheless, we still get angry. And it is so frustrating when the bull's-eye of this verse is in the back of my mind late at night, when Jennifer and I still haven't resolved an issue. I'm tired, I don't want to talk about my feelings anymore, and I just want to be left alone. But this is a trap being set, when it's not managed properly.

I know this is also something that coaches have a really hard time with. Between bad practices, losing close games, dealing with administration, and having to handle off-the-court issues, there are numerous things that a coach can come home with that haven't been dealt with. I think our human nature actually finds a twisted pleasure in letting our anger stew overnight like a Crock-Pot set to low. Whether it's a spouse, a child, a coworker, or a player, we must heed the guidance of Jesus about dealing with our anger before we go to sleep, because of what the fifth point is going to reveal.

5. *Don't give the devil an opportunity.* Something that I've learned through reading the Bible and hearing sermons is that Satan is constantly looking for entry points. Other translations of Mark 11 use the term "foothold" rather than opportunity. Because Satan is a spirit, he is always looking for areas that he can create confusion, doubt, or disbelief. A perfect example is the story of Adam and Eve in the garden in Genesis 3. When he approached Eve, who was instructed very clearly that they were not to eat of a particular tree or they would die, Satan's first question was, "Did God really say—?" He was searching for an entry point to deceive the woman of what she knew was a boundary. This is how the devil attacks us on a daily basis, and it's critical that you know this about your enemy!

We do the same thing in sports. Defensive coordinators spend all week watching possession after possession to try to find an entry point to disrupting the offense's scheme. Basketball coaches watch every shot the star player on the opposing team takes prior to their match up, in hopes that they will find a way to frustrate them and make them ineffective. In life, our enemy is Satan, and his objective is to make us ineffective for the kingdom of God. Anger is one of the entry points that Satan looks to attack us in, because everyone deals with anger. The reason why holding on to your anger is so dangerous is because it gives the devil an opportunity to get you to carry that bitterness into the next day of your life. If he can trap you in a cycle of anger, eventually he won't even need to worry about you anymore, because you will self-destruct all on your own. I believe there are some of you who have so much anger that has not been dealt with for so long that your life has become ineffective because you can't move past it. The emotional and physical distress that you deal with can only be overcome by the power of God and the blood of Jesus Christ that was shed on the cross for you. I pray that you will invite God into the broken places of your heart that have developed from anger in your past and that He would give you a fresh start!

There are many things in the game of basketball that can make us angry. There is cheating, lying, selfishness, unmet expectations, and much more that have the ability to get under our skin if we don't protect our thoughts. The first thing that I believe we have to do as *Sweet Sixteen* coaches is do a self-evaluation of our hearts into the areas we consistently find ourselves getting angry. Psalms 139 is an incredible example of this, and I would encourage you to read the whole chapter, but let's look at verses 23–24: "Search me, God, and know my heart; test me and know my anxious thoughts. See if there is any offensive way in me, and lead me in the way everlasting." For us to overcome this area in our lives, it starts with self-reflection and a humble attitude toward the God that knows our every thought.

The next thing I think needs to be done is we need to clear the air with anyone that we have resentment toward that affects us on a daily basis. We need to get the poison of bitterness out of us so we can truly start to get well. Then we need to begin to wash our minds with the Word of God. We need to think the way God thinks. We need to get to a place where we love what God loves and we have a distaste for what God hates. That takes a daily commitment to learning what His Word says. After that, I think the best thing you can do is take the situations that stir up anger in you moving forward and align them with these five checkpoints. I believe if we can live a life where we handle anger in these five ways, we will begin to see incredible things happen!

It's worth mentioning that 1 Corinthians 13 tells us something specific about our anger that I wanted to point out. It says that we are not to become *easily* angered. This is something that truly separates people who have control over their anger and people who don't. We've talked about everyone's personal battle with anger and how to deal with it appropriately, and this is a huge factor in that. An area that I see coaches missing the mark is how quickly they can become upset. I believe the stresses of winning and being responsible for young adults each day both play a big role in the short fuses of coaches, but it simply isn't acceptable. For whatever reason, we have deemed sports one of the few professions in life where it is socially acceptable for an adult to unleash their fury at kids and young adults. I think sometimes, what would happen to a bank manager if they unloaded their blind rage on their employees? My guess is they would be written up, possibly suspended, or maybe even fired immediately. I don't know why we have created a safe haven for coaches to act inappropriately toward impressionable and vulnerable youth, but it's extremely disappointing and not acceptable. As coaches, we need to work diligently on our tempers and not let ourselves become angered so easily.

I decided not to spend the majority of this chapter on coaches who yell and scream and have a very short temper because I think the issue with anger goes much deeper than a coach with a short fuse. We have talked already about coaches who blow off steam and belittle players as a coping mechanism for personal issues that they are working through, but I believe the Bible calls us to go deeper with the problem of anger. If you personally are struggling with blowing up at referees, your players, or even people in your house, I think it's important that you address that matter first. We are going to go through experiences in life regularly that test our ability to deal with anger in a way that is healthy and glorifies God. This is an area that God can receive so much honor, because of how challenging it is to deal with correctly. We need to keep in mind that God tells us to call Him Abba Father, which refers to an intimate relationship between a father and his child. He wants us to have a relationship with Him the way that a child does with their dad. He created us in a way where we would *have to* rely on Him to live an exceptional life. When we try to get these places of our lives cleaned up on our own, it's like a child trying to learn how to ride a bike without training wheels alone. Let God support you in your battle with anger, because He cares for you! You'll have a lot fewer crashes, I can promise you that.

> My dear brothers and sisters, take note of this: Everyone should be quick to listen, slow to speak and slow to become angry, because human anger does not produce the righteousness that God desires. (James 1:19–20, NIV)

> Fools give full vent to their rage, but the wise bring calm in the end. (Proverbs 29:11, NIV)

> Do not be quickly provoked in your spirit, for anger resides in the lap of fools. (Ecclesiastes 7:9, NIV)

> But now you must also rid yourselves of all such things as these: anger, rage, malice, slander, and filthy language from your lips. (Colossians 3:8, NIV)

> Do not make friends with a hot-tempered person, do not associate with one easily angered. (Proverbs 22:24, NIV)

Chapter 10

It Keeps No Record of Wrongs

In sports, your record is everything. The two numbers separated by a dash next to your team's name tells the story of your season. We care so much about our record. For some coaches, it defines them. Over the past six years, it's been interesting to see how different people emphasize their record. Personally, there are times throughout the year that when someone asks me what our record is, I couldn't tell them the answer. I would genuinely have to guess, and I would probably be off by a game or two. I know some coaches that could tell you every team's record in the whole conference off the top of their head. It's actually quite impressive! I've never been wired that way, with the exception of a few teams I've been on, when we were undefeated for a significant portion of the season.

Regardless of whether you are the type to remember records or you're like me and you don't usually pay attention, the one thing that can be said about records is in every sport, they keep them. If you spend any time watching collegiate or professional sports, you at some point have heard the color commentators bring up facts, information, and statistics that are mind-blowingly specific. It's amazing what things we have recorded over the history of sports. Sometimes I have to laugh at the stats they bring up, because it seems obnoxious to be able to recall some of the things that announcers will discuss. Naturally, my friends and I over the years have had fun exaggerating some of the random facts that we assume we will hear prior to an event that we are about to watch such as, "You know, if LeBron James and the Lakers find a way to pull of this win tonight in Boston, it will only be the fifth time since the implementation of the three-point line that the Lakers won on the road, against an East Conference team in February, on a Monday night, while wearing their gold uniforms." What! How could someone possibly have enough stored information to know that? But more importantly, who cares?

The truth is we care. There's something about knowing as much information as possible about a game, a player, or an event that makes us feel connected to the athletes and helps us predict the outcome. We base so many of our predictions, assumptions, and beliefs off records. And I think this makes sports enjoyable for fans. There's nothing like getting that March Madness bracket in your hands, as you scour the Internet for every statistic you can find to help you make the perfect bracket. There are millions of dollars exchanging hands in Las Vegas on a daily basis, as people try to use records and data to predict spreads. The place that this becomes a determent is when we decide to keep records of people's past mistakes so we can deliver a guilty verdict.

I will start by saying that this is one of the toughest areas of love for me, in *The Sweet Sixteen*. If it were up to me, I would request that we cut it down to fifteen and have this one omitted. I struggle with this issue on a constant basis, not only when dealing with my players but also in all my relationships. My wife would tell you I have an impressive memory, and she would also tell you that sometimes she wishes that I didn't. When there is an issue in our relationship, I quickly transform into the all-time great announcer, Jim Nantz, as I calmly remind Jennifer of every infraction she's made in the area of discussion in great detail. It doesn't matter if it was over two years ago, most likely I can describe everything about the moment in question down to the shoes we had on. This has been an area of contention in our relationship, as you can imagine, because I have a hard time showing *agape* in this area. The thing I want you to know is that most of us aren't going to be awful at every trait in *The Sweet Sixteen*. Typically, we are going to have a couple that will quickly identify as our Achilles' heel. It's important that we humbly identify those weaknesses so God can do the mighty work He desires to do.

I think sports caters to this misunderstanding of God's love. In sports, we applaud the ability to remember records, both good and bad, as something to be celebrated. As a coach and a player, we make the majority of our decisions based off past records. It dictates how we perceive people, and we knowingly or unknowingly put people in imaginary boxes. For us to love people, we will have to remove this pattern of thinking that we use in sports to predict outcomes and live a life of fresh starts. This will not be easy to do, but I believe this verse will help give some perspective.

> Praise the LORD, my soul; all my inmost being, praise his holy name. Praise the LORD, my soul, and forget not all his benefits—who forgives all your sins and heals all your diseases, who redeems your life from the pit and crowns you with love and compassion, who satisfies your desires with good things so that your youth is renewed like the eagle's. The LORD works righteousness and justice for all the oppressed. He made known his ways to Moses, his deeds to the people of Israel: The LORD is compassionate and gracious, slow to anger, abounding in love. He will not always accuse, nor will he harbor his anger forever; he does not treat us as our sins deserve or repay us according to our iniquities. For as high as the heavens are above the earth, so great is his love for those who fear him; as far as the east is from the west, so far has he removed our transgressions from us. (Psalms 103:1–12, NIV)

When I think about the hard time I have forgetting the wrongs that have been done to me, it seems like a pretty daunting and painful process. Real hurts are hard to get over. Then I read this chapter and am slapped in the face with the reality that the number of times I've hurt God, who died for me before I even knew Him, is countless and He not only forgives me but also says He forgets them. Talk about being humbled.

I can't help but laugh at how the order of *The Sweet Sixteen* has us deal with not keeping records of wrongs, right after dealing with anger. Then we read what David, the writer of Psalms 103, said about how our God loves us and he makes it clear that "the LORD is compassionate and gracious, slow to anger, abounding in love. He will not always accuse, nor will he harbor his anger forever; he does not treat us as our sins deserve or repay us according to our iniquities." God expresses how He loves us by not letting the sun go down on His anger toward us and then doesn't treat us according to our sin. Our God is so consistent at setting the example for how He calls us to live so we don't have to step out on a limb, but we merely have to follow His example. Not only does God's anger last for a short time, but also when you know the significance of why He used the distinction between east and west, I believe it will change your life.

If you read the *Book of Mysteries* by Johnathan Cahn, you will learn that before knowledge that the earth wasn't flat, God established the east–west continuum with the Israelites. The Hebrew word for east is *kedem*, which also means everlasting. The temple of Jerusalem was built according to the *kedem*. It had to face the east. The altar of the sacrifice was at its easternmost end. The holy of holies was at its westernmost end. Everything else was in between. Everything in the temple existed and took place on an east–west continuum. Most importantly, on the holiest day of the year, *Yom Kippur*, the sins of Israel were atoned for and removed from the people.

The high priest would offer up the sacrifice in the east and then sprinkle the blood on the ark of the covenant in the west. He would journey back and forth on the east–west continuum, and the closing act of the day would be seeing the sins of the people symbolically removed from the west to the east.

This is significant because the earth is actually a sphere, and it turns on its axis on an east–west continuum. Therefore, the earth has a north pole and a south pole, but no east or west pole. Since there are two poles both north and south, the distance between the two is limited. All north comes to an end at the north pole, and all south comes to an end at the south pole. If the temple had been built on a north–south continuum, then that would have implied that there was a limit to how far sin could only be removed from the sinner. However, east and west have no poles. Therefore, they never end. East and west are infinite. They go on forever.

Before human beings even knew the structure of our globe, God made a commitment to them that He would remove our sins infinitely! At the time that this promise was being made, there was no real significance to the promise. We now are able to see how incredible our God is and how radically He desires to forgive us when we make mistakes.

God bears such a higher price in regard to forgiveness, and yet He does it with a love and grace that is indescribable. I don't know about you, but when I read the way God forgives me, it compels me to get rid of my prideful selfishness when I hold people's wrongs against them.

In basketball, there are mistakes made all the time, both from a relationship standpoint and on the court. And because we, as coaches, have committed ourselves to a career that promises us a lifetime of wrongs committed, it's important that we talk about how we can overcome the eagerness to hold on tightly to those mistakes. The two most destructive ways I see coaches mishandle this call to love people when it comes to keeping record of wrongs are *holding onto offenses* and *putting conditions* on our willingness show kindness.

Holding on to Offenses

We have a hard time as human beings letting things go. We might not be able to remember what we had for lunch last Tuesday, but we can certainly recall an offense that happened months before that. This is something we must battle on a daily basis in regard to our athletes. When it comes to off-the-court issues of any kind, as coaches, we need to anticipate controversy with our players. The fact of the matter is players are going to make mistakes. They're human, and humans screw up. It's also important to remember that each one of your players has a lifetime of habits (potentially bad habits) that have formed outside of your control from their homelife. You may have a player on your team that tends to lie about everything to avoid getting in trouble. You might have a player who really struggles to wake up on time and has a bad habit of being late to stuff. I've dealt with players cheating on homework and tests on multiple occasions. The thing to remember is most young adults don't start these behaviors once they're a part of your program. These are habits they've developed over the course of their life.

It is critical that standards are set on your team where there are consequences for actions of misconduct, such as these, because no successful program allows players to step out of line without repercussions. What a *Sweet Sixteen* coach is called to do is not punish players for past infractions that have already been dealt with but more importantly not hold a grudge over previous mistakes—things like, "I received an e-mail from your teacher saying he had suspicions about you cheating on homework. I assume you were, since this wouldn't be the first time you've been accused of this." "The baseball coach said they're missing some Gatorade from their locker room. I know you've stolen things in the past, so I had a hunch that you were involved."

These examples show an inability to let the past be the past. By constantly keeping a record book of a player's poor decisions, you define their future based on their prior mistakes. You never give them space to change and become a better person. I think we do that because we want to protect ourselves. There is an element of not wanting to be hurt by someone again that pushes us to assume the worst. If we assume our player was guilty and it comes out that they weren't, then it's a pleasant surprise. If we trust them, in spite of their past mistakes, and the truth comes out that they were in the wrong, we allow ourselves to be hurt. *Agape* can only be shown when we take the risk of being hurt in order to love someone unconditionally.

The scary part about this mind-set is that it's common for people who are always judged by their past to give up trying to change. They get so worn out from fighting their own deficiencies while being beat down verbally that they decide it's just easier to be who everyone thinks they are. I pray that I am never an enabler of one of my athletes thinking like that. I desire for my willingness to keep no record of wrong to give them hope for tomorrow and hope in themselves.

Coaches also get in the habit of keeping record of wrongs on the court. I do think this is a much harder place to navigate, because basketball is about results. If a post player wants to bring the ball up the floor and can't dribble very well, it's simply unwise to let them because you don't want to keep a record of their inability to dribble. When dealing with holding on to offenses on the court, the focus needs to be centered on the *hope* that we provide them.

Every player has a max potential and a place they are currently at. The gap between the two will vary from player to player. I believe the best coaches are the ones who both teach and encourage a player in a way that helps them max out their potential. This becomes almost impossible when we keep a record of wrongs. Players must be given a healthy dose of both encouragement and reality checks. Failing to do either of these can limit the potential of a player.

Kids naturally gravitate toward what they see as being popular, and in basketball today, being a perimeter player is popular. Shooting threes, crossing people over, and throwing no-look passes are what catches an audience's attention and therefore are what kids want to develop into. The problem is there are a small percentage of basketball players who can successfully do those things, while there are hundreds, if not thousands, trying to add them to their game. As *Sweet Sixteen* coaches, we need to know the game and our players well enough to see what role they would be most successful in both personally and for the overall success of the team. It is then our responsibility to paint that picture to them clearly so they have the opportunity to grow into the best version of that player.

It is also the responsibility of a *Sweet Sixteen* coach to find ways to encourage a player's creativity. Players will always have a desire to add things to their game. Sometimes it's beneficial, and in other cases, it is a waste of time. Great coaches have the ability to keep players focused on growing inside the boundaries of the player they are being asked to be while also encouraging them to add other skills to their game when they've spent the appropriate time developing those skills. This is the tightrope that a lot of coaches fall off. If you let your players do whatever they want, then there's really no reason to have a coach. Your purpose is to develop a team who individually knows their best assets, strives to be the best version of that player, and knows how to work together with their teammates to function at maximum capacity. A coach who lets players decide what is best for the team, especially in basketball, will *always* struggle to be consistent. Players need a coach who sets parameters and demands that each person stay inside the boundaries of their role.

The place where *holding on to offenses* happens on the court is when a coach refuses to ever let a player try to develop any other skills than they already have. Coaches who stifle their team's creativity, in my opinion, are failing just as much as coaches who have no discipline. The reason I've seen coaches deter their players from working on new areas of their game is because of what they know about the player. They've seen how bad of a shooter they are from behind the three-point line. They remember what happened the last time they tried to create a shot off the dribble and lost the ball out-of-bounds. Coaches don't soon forget how horrible a player's free throw percentage is when they ask to have the ball in their hands at the end of the game when the other team is fouling.

When a player is driven and excited about developing their game, we need to encourage that drive! We live in a day and age where trying to get young adults to be motivated to do *anything* that doesn't involve being on their phone is a challenge. One of the ways that energizes young athletes to work harder and put in extra time is by encouraging their passion to get better. How we screw this up is when we are so against the things they want to work on that we shut the whole thing down and tell them to stop practicing. I believe *Sweet Sixteen* coaches can use that passion and find compromises with their players to support their desire to get better but still keep them inside the boundaries.

Let's use the three situations that I brought up. If a historically bad shooter on your team wants to have the green light to shoot the ball, the first thing that needs to be done is they need to know the truth about their shooting ability. Whether that's having a straightforward conversation about their shooting form or looking at their percentages or both, they need to know that you're not just against the idea for no reason. The next thing you can do is find places on the court and situations that you would be comfortable with them developing their shooting ability, if they were willing to put the time in. Make sure they know specifically what those shots and situations are and give them a workout plan so they know how to improve. It's most important that you tell them once they've consistently worked to get better that the two of you will reevaluate whether they've improved enough to have the green light.

By doing this, you have given them something to be passionate about and work hard for. You've also shown that you *want* to see them continue to develop as a player, but you get to determine what that looks like within your system.

With a player who wants to create their own shot, I think you first need to determine if that's a role that you want them to have. Maybe they're the type of player where the answer is yes, but within very strict parameters. That's perfectly fine. Those parameters just need to be defined. Take some time and evaluate how they are most effective scoring the ball and if you can find a way to implement that into your offense. If they do one or two moves particularly well, try putting them in situations in practice where they have the opportunity to score using those moves. If it goes well, then that might be something you need to try in a game. If it doesn't go well, then you have concrete feedback you can discuss with the athlete.

If they are a player that isn't ready for that role yet, a great way to handle the situation is to give them one or two moves that you would like to see them develop for the next season. Have them work on the move(s) outside of practice or in workouts over the course of the off-season so the following year, they are ready to implement those into their game.

When dealing with a player who struggles from the free throw line, again, there needs to be a very intentional conversation about *why* they shouldn't have the ball at the end of the game. As much as we don't want to believe this about our players, there are some athletes who genuinely don't think about the big picture like we do as coaches. The good thing about free throws is they aren't subjective like a lot of things in basketball. When the game is on the line in the last few minutes and the opponent has no choice but to foul, it's imperative that the best free throw shooters have the ball in their hands. Once again, it's so valuable to have honest, transparent conversations with your players, because it shows them that you earnestly consider the things they talk to you about. I would recommend setting a percentage that you want players to shoot from the line for them to be on the floor in late-game situations. Or maybe, it's not a matter of being on the floor, but who the ball needs to go to as soon as your team has possession. Like the other two scenarios that we've brought up, set that expectation with your player, and give them ways to grow into that player. You could give them a free throw workout to do daily or talk to them about the mental aspect of free throws and find out if there's something that's hindering them that's not physically related. Personally, I like to do minigames or situations in practice where players have to shoot live free throws so they simulate the real pressure of hitting two from the line.

The theme I want you to take away from each of these examples is the understanding that we are meant to provide *hope*. It's important that your team plays by the guidelines that you set for them, but we also must be proactive in finding ways to keep our players energized and excited about developing. There is no substitute for the belief and encouragement of a coach.

Putting Conditions on Our Kindness

I see this take place on teams regularly. I see this happen in relationships outside of sports as well. This is an area that can be very damaging to a relationship between a player and coach, and I believe it shows signs of immaturity. The reason I think it shows immaturity is because toddlers are wired this way. When a kid at preschool takes their toy, they gravitate toward holding that infraction over their head. As we grow up and mature, this is an area where we need to stop acting like a child. We talked at length in chapter 4 about kindness and how it's becoming a lost virtue in our society. One of the things that ruins a coaches' desire to be kind is the record book of wrongs that they have in the filing cabinet of their minds. Most people would define this as holding a grudge.

When your kindness, as a coach, becomes part of the *terms and conditions* of your relationship with your team, you have set your team up for a roller-coaster experience. You won't find a team at any level or any sport that doesn't struggle to be successful. It's part of the beauty of sports. Teams relish the sweet taste of victory because they've experienced the bitterness of defeat. This is why all losses aren't always a bad thing. Losing is what makes winning enjoyable!

As coaches, we need to determine that we are going to see the best in our players regardless of their mistakes and shortcomings. They need to have the freedom to fail forward. Knowing that they are inevitably going to fail, they need to be able to do so without fear of it going on their permanent record. Over the years of being a player, I learned the internal pressure of trying to perform with the fear of my mistakes having long-lasting consequences. I remember not caring nearly as much about the result of an error, in regard to the outcome of the game, as much as how long the mistake would be tattooed on my coaches' impression of me.

The following is a list of ways coaches put conditions on their kindness:

- Showing up to practice already upset with everyone, because of an e-mail the coach received about one individual on the team earlier that morning
- Making the comment, "If you guys want me to stop yelling at you, then make a layup for once and I'll stop!"
- Not starting a player after they've had a string of bad games, without ever explaining to them why their playing time has significantly change with the assumption, "They'll figure it out."
- Getting to eat healthy meals on the road when you're winning and then telling your team they have a $5 limit at a fast-food restaurant, after a poor performance
- Deciding that the team will practice at 5:00 a.m. that will consist of only running and defense since, "We don't do anything else well, so we might as well get in shape."

Earlier, we talked about the definition of *agape* and how it is the highest form of love, because it is unconditional. I believe it is the highest form of love, because it costs the giver the highest price. I am not saying that it is easy to throw away the record book of mistakes. I'm actually attesting to how difficult it is! You will continue to see a theme throughout the call of a *Sweet Sixteen* coach that will ask you to truly sacrifice all that you have to achieve this incomparable bond of love. One of the things that encourages me on this journey is that we are always faced with areas that need to be improved. In the same way that our players hear us call out their deficiencies, as we try to help them succeed, God's Word does the same thing with us!

The other thing that gives me hope and encouragement always comes back to my relationship with God. I know how often I screw up. I'm aware of the horrible things I think and struggle with that other people don't have access to. But knowing that my Father in heaven knows my deepest thoughts and keeps no record of my wrongs compels me to live the same way. Luke 7:36–50 tells a story of a woman whose sins were made known to the public, and she came before Jesus and offered an extravagant expression of worship. While the self-righteous people around her looked down on her sin, Jesus was astonished by her willingness to humble herself before Him and the judgmental people. Verse 47 says, "I tell you, her sins—and they are many—have been forgiven, so she has sown me much love. But a person who is forgiven little shows only little love."

A *Sweet Sixteen* coach should evaluate the innermost struggles of their heart and understand the realness of this verse. We have been forgiven of so much! How can we not be compelled to turn around and forgive much? You'll notice as you read these scriptures that God repeatedly uses Himself as the standard to live by. I pray coaches everywhere would forgive, as we have been forgiven.

> For if you forgive other people when they sin against you, your heavenly Father will also forgive you. But if you do not forgive others their sins, your Father will not forgive your sins. (Matthew 6:14–15, NIV)

Be kind and compassionate to one another, forgiving each other, just as in Christ God forgave you. (Ephesians 4:32, NIV)

So watch yourselves. "If your brother or sister sins against you, rebuke them; and if they repent, forgive them. Even if they sin against you seven times in a day and seven times come back to you saying 'I repent,' you must forgive them." (Luke 17:3–4, NIV)

Sensible people control their temper; they earn respect by overlooking wrongs. (Proverbs 19:11, NLT)

Don't speak evil against each other, dear brothers and sisters. If you criticize and judge each other, then you are criticizing and judging God's law. But your job is to obey the law, not to judge whether it applies to you. God alone, who gave the law, is the Judge. He alone has the power to save or to destroy. So what right do you have to judge your neighbor? (James 4:11–12, NLT)

Chapter 11

Love Does Not Delight in Evil but Rejoices in the Truth

As I stood on the sidelines that Friday night, the sounds of shoulder pads colliding and the sweet smell of one of the locals smoking a pipe behind the sidelines is what I remember most. As a freshman on the football team, I was named the starting QB for our first game against West Branch High School. Due to a horrific first half and a senior QB who was undoubtedly more mature than I was, I ended up riding the bench for the duration of the season. On that particular Friday, we were playing a home game against one of the most feared 1A teams in the state of Iowa, North Mahaska.

For the majority of small school, it's very common to have undersized athletes. As a senior basketball player, I was the tallest guy in our starting lineup on the court, standing at six feet tall. The thing is it seemed normal because everyone was small, so we didn't think anything of it. But not the Hawks of North Mahaska. Watching their offense jog onto the field from the opposing sideline gave you a similar feeling to seeing someone's older brother walk into a room to handle a problem someone had with his younger sibling. They were *huge*! In a league where most offensive linemen typically didn't surpass 6'2" and 215 pounds, North Mahaska's boys up front looked like they could have tried out for the New York Jets.

While their linemen were incredibly intimidating, it paled in comparison to their star player and running back, Levi Ferguson. Levi wasn't like the rest of us "small-town Iowa kids." Levi looked like he was put together in a laboratory somewhere. He was fast, strong, could run circles around anyone big enough to bring him down, and leave the outline of a smaller player's body in the grass if they got between him and the goal line. He was arguably the most impressive athlete in Class 1A in the whole state. He most likely would have gone on to play running back at a Division 1 school somewhere, if he hadn't been even better at baseball. To this day, I still wonder if the rumor that he was being recruited by the White Sox out of high school was true.

Watching him play football was a sight to see. I didn't have the privilege of growing up in a big city where the athletic talent was superb. I was a good athlete, all things considered, but nothing like this kid. He was a special athlete, and I was thrilled to have been observing his talent from the sidelines that night and wasn't responsible for attempting to tackle Goliath. Otherwise, I might not be writing this book today!

The events that took place that night will forever be engrained into my head about the character of my head coach, Chad Edeker, and the way competition has made us lose sight of *agape*. It was midway through the first half, and North Mahaska had the ball and were marching down the field. They ran their patented stretch iso for Levi to get him to the outside, and as he broke past the first level of defenders, he was met by our middle linebacker. As he went down to the ground, after only picking up three or four yards, a loud cheer from the sidelines and the bleachers roared through the cool night air. Holding Levi to less than a first down every carry was a praiseworthy accomplishment. What happened next is where the story took a turn. As the pile was clearing off the ground, Levi lay there clearly in pain, gripping the back of his leg. He had severely strained his hamstring. The fact that he was even susceptible to injury like the rest of us didn't even seem possible. But as he laid there in pain, it was as if my thoughts and my teammates' reaction were synced up to the same Wi-Fi. As he rolled back and forth grimacing in pain while the trainer ran out to check on him, all I could think to myself was, *Levi is hurt! We're going to win!* Although no words came out of my mouth, my heart was overjoyed with the thought of a Levi-less opponent. Unfortunately, there were about twenty to thirty of my teammates that weren't so quick to keep their thoughts to themselves and started clapping and cheering even louder at the sight of the Hawks' secret weapon suffering.

Everyone's excitement about our chances of winning skyrocketing was drowned out by Coach Edeker turning around and *screaming* at the top of his lungs, "Hey! I better not ever hear one more person cheer about someone getting hurt, or you'll be off this team!" We were shook. I don't know that I had ever seen coach so infuriated before. You could have heard a pin drop. That moment has stuck with me for over a decade. The reason why is because I realized in that moment winning a high school football game became more important to me than the health of another human being. And even though zero words came out of my mouth in that moment, in my heart, I was happy to see him injured. This is a major problem that we have *learned* in our culture, and it is spreading like cancer through our sports. Levi, if you ever read this, I want to apologize from the bottom of my heart. I did not represent the God that I serve. I hope life is going well for you!

*****

1 Corinthians 13 in other translations says, "It does not rejoice in wrongdoing." Wrongdoing has unfortunately become a cornerstone in sports today. People are willing to do *whatever* it takes to win. If lying, cheating, or stealing will get us to the winner's circle, then it's worth it. "If you ain't cheatin', you ain't tryin'!" has become the mantra of sports. If a coach has to cuss out the team to get them to pay attention, then so be it. From performance-enhancing drugs, paying college athletes under the table, using sex and prostitution to entice a commit to sign, to high school teachers not submitting the grades of their star athlete until the season is over so they can stay eligible, we have really got it twisted. I think the scariest part of this

corrupt area is that not only is it happening, but also we have gotten to a place where we not only find ourselves participating in some of these activities but also *delight* in them! Instead of being ashamed and remorseful of our motives, we have started feeling good about them. Our understanding of love is slowly being perverted. Our lust for victory is swallowing up our ability to truly love.

There are so many evil and wrong things that are happening in sports today that it would be impossible to name all of them or even put them in categories. Sports are the perfect climate to incubate evil motives and actions. What I want to address is what the second half of this call to love says, "But rejoices in the truth." Another translation says, "But rejoices when the truth wins out." This is such a good translation for us as coaches, because if there's one thing that we relate to, it's winning. I'm sure most of you have been to a game and when it was over and you were discussing the outcome the statement, "I think it's wrong that _____ ended up winning that game" has come out of someone's mouth. I know I've felt that way dozens of times. There are multiple different reasons that we might feel that the team who lost didn't *deserve* to lose, but the mind-set is all the same. Something about how the game went made us, as an outside observer, feel that the team who lost deserved to win out.

As a *Sweet Sixteen* coach, God desires to see us delight when the truth wins over anything else—even if that anything else is winning. I believe this starts with a heart that truly loves God. Truth is something that gets tossed around quite a bit, and I think it's often mistaken for fact. As much as we subscribe to trusting in facts, facts have the potential to change. As our world grows and changes and we learn more, facts change. Truth, on the other hand, will never change. Jesus said in John 14:6, "I am the way, the Truth, and the life." In John 1, we read that Jesus the man was in existence before He took on His human body and was known as the Word.

> In the beginning was the Word, and the Word was with God, and the Word was God. He was with God in the beginning. Through him all things were made; without him nothing was made that

has been made. In him was life, and that life was the light of all mankind. The light shines in the darkness, and the darkness has not overcome it.

This is why later in John 1, it says, "The Word became flesh and made his dwelling among us." Jesus, long before having the name that we know Him as, was actually known as the Word. Ironically, we also refer to the Bible as God's Word. What does this mean? It means that the Word of God, the Bible, is the only thing on earth that is truth. Everything outside of the Word of God (both the man Jesus and the book left for us) may be factual, but it is not truth. This is very difficult to believe, but it is imperative for Christ-followers to put their faith in. Hebrews 13:8 says, "Jesus Christ is the same yesterday and today and forever." Can you think of *anything* else in life that you can say confidently is the same yesterday, today, and forever? That is why truth is so powerful and why the life of a Christ-follower is so wonderful. We have a firm foundation that we can rely on without worrying if culture, year, president, or scientific data will change.

Now that we look back at this command of love, we can understand it with more understanding. God says that true love is not delighting in evil, but rejoicing in Him and His Word. Wrongdoing and the Bible are polar opposites. To show *agape* toward the players on our team, we must know the truth and rejoice when it wins out—not only when it wins out around us but also when it wins out *in* us. I believe that this is next to impossible when we don't have a true desire to follow and please God. The reason why is because there are a lot of things in life that are going to get messy and complicated when we choose truth. We might lose a game, we might lose our job, or we might find our circle of friends become increasing smaller. There will eventually be a price to pay for choosing truth, but know this, the price you pay will come here on earth, and your reward will come in eternity. If you choose to avoid paying the price of truth during your life on this earth, you will find that the interest that you pay once this life is over is costly.

What does this look like on a daily basis in our world? The first thing that it requires is that you discipline yourself to learn what the

Bible says. How can you know the answers to a test if you never look at the study guide? Every day we are faced with tests, from whether you should cut a corner to make things easier on yourself, or if you should speak up when you see something inappropriate happening, or just stay out of it so you don't have to deal with the repercussions. If there's one thing that I've learned in the few years that I've been coaching is that you will constantly have opportunities to speak up for truth or choose not to get involved.

I am reminded of the commercial where a basketball goes out-of-bounds and the referee gives it to one team as both teams go over for a time-out. The player who was closest to it interrupts what his coach is saying and says, "Coach, I touched it." The coach asks him what he said, and he repeats, "I touched it." The coach smiles at him with the proud look of a father and says, "All right." The coach gave him the go-ahead to let the referee know that they got the call wrong, and it was actually out-of-bounds off him. I've actually watched that commercial with a group of friends who have said, "That dude is an idiot! I hope that lost them the game. I would never do that." And it made me realize how *true* God's Word is. Rejoicing in the truth winning out is guaranteed to cause conflict in your life. The question is, are you prepared for that?

On the other side of the coin, I think of the times I've been watching pro sports, and because of the number of cameras that are involved in sports today, the TV viewers don't miss anything. I can vividly recall both an NBA game and an NFL game where a player got away with something that they knew the referees missed. The basketball player was in a similar situation as the commercial and knocked a ball out-of-bounds and the ref gave the ball to them. In the football game, a defensive back went to defend a pass thrown across the middle and batted the ball away cleanly but egregiously held the wide receiver with his other arm and the ref missed it. In both plays, the audience booed and demanded they show a replay so justice would be served. Both replays had evidence that the referee missed their respected calls, but what was so troublesome about the plays was that both players who knew they got away with something they shouldn't have had almost identical smug smiles on their face as they lavished the thought of getting away with something they shouldn't have. While some of you might think this isn't a big deal, I would like us to ask ourselves what the ramifications of this happening game after game will be. The question, "I wonder what else I can get away with?" is bound to come up in the player's mind eventually.

Evilness is a gradual process. Very few people go from 0 to 100 when it comes to wrongdoing. They slowly become conditioned to a little bit of evil, and it eventually doesn't seem that bad. The person becomes numb to what used to make their heart race when they tried it, and months later, doing something that they used to think was horrible isn't outside the realm of possibilities. We must guard our hearts with all diligence because evil is always lurking outside the door, waiting for someone to answer the persistent knocking. When we rejoice in the truth, because we know what the truth is, we mentally lock the doors of our heart from the enemy getting in.

When it comes to your relationship with your team, this life-changing principle starts with you yourself cleaning up the areas in your life that you find yourself choosing evil over truth. We must examine ourselves and be honest about places that we're willing to compromise what's right for what's easy. After we are willing to do that, we can now seek to impart that into our players. I believe the best way to do this is by following this verse very literally. When you see your players doing something wrong, not making a mistake, but actually participating in evil, it's crucial that you not delight in it. Even if it's funny or benefits the team, it has to be handled strictly. The second thing, and this is where we have to be intentional, is we need to *rejoice* when the truth wins out in our players. It's really easy to see our players do something that is a great example of this verse, and we just think to ourselves that we're happy they did that. We need to *rejoice*! In the same way that we celebrate winning competitions, we need to celebrate when our players choose truth. Human beings are drawn to praise. We soak it up like a sponge and do whatever we can to recreate it so we can receive more praise. By setting the example of not delighting in evil, but rejoicing in the truth and then rejoicing when your players choose truth, you are creating an environment that will change the culture of your team! Not only will you change the culture, but also you will be a part of changing their lives.

The Bible has a lot to say about both avoiding evil and pursuing truth and righteousness. Use these verses to start learning and memorizing truth so you can be prepared when you're faced with tough decisions in your job.

> Test all things; hold fast to what is good. Abstain from every form of evil. (1 Thessalonians 5:21–22, NKJV)

> Do not waste time arguing over godless ideas and old wives' tales. Instead, train yourself to be godly. Physical training is good, but training for godliness is much better, promising benefits in this life and in the life to come. (1 Timothy 4:7–8, NLT)

> Dear friends, I warn you as "temporary residents and foreigners" to keep away from worldly desires that wage war against your very souls. Be careful to live properly among your unbelieving neighbors. Then even if they accuse you of doing wrong, they will see your honorable behavior, and they will give honor to God when he judges the world. (1 Peter 2:11–12, NLT)

> Work hard so you can present yourself to God and receive approval. Be a good worker, one who does not need to be ashamed and correctly explains the word of truth. Avoid worthless, foolish talk that only leads to more godless behavior. (2 Timothy 2:15–16)

> Therefore, put on every piece of God's armor so you will be able to resist the enemy in the time of

evil. Then after the battle you will still be stand-ing firm. Stand your ground, putting on the belt of truth and the body armor of God's righteous-ness. (Ephesians 6:13–14, NLT)

But the time is coming-indeed it's here now-when true worshipers will worship the Father in spirit and in truth. The Father is looking for those who will worship him that way. For God is Spirit, so those who worship him must worship in spirit and in truth. (John 4:23–24, NLT)

Chapter 12

It Always Protects

I t was week two of my freshman year at Iowa Western, back when
I played football. All throughout spring ball and summer camp,
I was confident that I would get the starting spot at quarterback
come week one. Unfortunately, as we got closer to our home opener
and inaugural game of Iowa Western's football team, I was named
the backup behind David Blackwell. It was a tough pill to swallow,
knowing that I did everything I could, and felt I was prepared to
start, only to find myself standing on the sidelines week one.

We struggled the first game of the season against a solid, run-
heavy Iowa Central team and had to refocus for the next opponent
coming to our home field. Joliet Junior College, out of Chicago,
Illinois, was a very talented team, and we would have to get over our
loss to Iowa Central quickly. Our offense wasn't great that opening
Saturday afternoon, so naturally I was in my head the next three days
wondering if Coach Stroh would be reconsidering the QB position.
Coach Scott Strohmeier and I had a great relationship, and to this
day, I think he is one of the most genuine, compassionate people I've
ever played for. He wasn't just a great football coach, who knew his
X's and O's; he cared about you as a person, didn't try to scare you
into playing well, and always seemed to have a positive attitude.

I never had any animosity for Coach Stroh about choosing to
start David, but I always questioned what I had done wrong or what
more I needed to do for him to choose me. My mom instilled hard

work and a never-give-up attitude in me, so I showed up to practice the next week with the mind-set that if I was given a shot the following week, I would be ready.

I have always been very detail oriented, almost to a fault. I am extremely meticulous about the smallest things and have always been that way. This has helped me in sports tremendously, because I believe winning is in the details. I would spend at least ten hours per week in a classroom, with or without Coach Stroh, watching film. I would watch every rep I ever took in practice and rewatch it at least five times. I would breakdown my footwork in the pocket to figure out how I could perfect my balance. I would study my arm motion and compare it to some of my favorite QBs to learn how I could get the ball out quicker. Then I would watch the defensive backfield to find any and all presnap tips I could gather to give me the slightest advantage once the ball was in my hands.

I was obsessed. God designed me to love details. The smallest things are the biggest things to me. I loved sitting down in front of a screen, in a dark room, with a control in my hand and the desire to mentally become the best player I could be. Coach Stroh and I would typically meet up once or twice a week to sit down and watch our next opponent's defense, to make sure we were on the same page about the game plan and how we wanted to attack them. It was so fun for me to discuss route concepts and defensive coverages and feel like I was on the same wavelength with my coach. Even though I had never even considered the idea of coaching at that time in my life, now being in my sixth year of collegiate coaching, I hope that I provide the same sense of closeness to my players as Scott did for me.

Early in the season, even though I wasn't playing, I prepared myself as though I was the starter. The belief that my time was going to come and that I had to be prepared for the moment when it arrived pushed me to think like a starter. Week two would end up being my chance.

Saturday afternoon came, and I was still in the role of backup QB. The game went back and forth, and nobody ever took a commanding lead. Our offense struggled yet again, and we couldn't seem to get any momentum. Deep into the third quarter, we had back-to-back turnovers, and the moment I had been waiting for was about to show up. Coach Stroh came over to me right after the offense jogged off the field and said the words I had been waiting for, "Austin, get ready. You're going in next drive."

I don't know if you've ever experienced the pre-roller-coaster feeling, where half of you is excited after all the anticipation and the other half of you is terrified that you committed to it, but that's the feeling I experienced. I spent every day training, studying, and preparing for this very moment; and as I heard my name called, I immediately had doubts.

I jogged over to grab a ball from the QB bag and started warming up my arm with one of the wide receivers. I attempted to regurgitate all the information I had studied on Joliet's pass coverages, like sitting down to a final exam after cramming the night before. My mind was completely blank. I knew I just had to get out onto the field and let my instincts take control.

Joliet punted, and it was finally my turn. We jogged over to Coach Stroh, and he called our first play. He was smart enough to know that I would be nervous and called a run plan. We got lined up, and I scanned the secondary trying to recognize what I'd seen on film. Everything in that moment seemed completely brand new, as if I had prepared for the wrong team. I specifically remember looking at the defensive line and felt like I was right back in Wayland, Iowa, under the Friday night lights. These dudes were huge! And their main objective for the rest of the game was to take my helmet off.

After collecting my thoughts, I shouted, "White 80! White 80! Set hut!" The ball spiraled back to me and I tucked it in the chest of my running back, Kevis Streeter. It was a read option, so my assignment was to read the defensive end, who by design went unblocked. If he commits to the running back, I keep it. If he stays in his gap, I hand it off. The defensive end stayed at home, so I gave it to Kevis and faked like I kept it. The first four steps I took felt like I was moving 100 mph! Adrenaline and anxiousness were coursing through my body. Kevis picked up a solid gain of seven or eight yards, and I felt like I could finally relax. My first collegiate play was in the books. No fumbles, no interceptions, no loss of yards. Whew!

I looked over at Stroh, and he signaled to run the same play. Gaining another three yards and getting a first down would bring a lot of ease to our squad. I called the same play, broke the huddle, and walked to the line. With a much clearer head, I scanned the field again and finally felt like I was back on the practice field. I called the cadence, the ball was snapped, and I got my eyes right on the defensive end once more. He stayed in his gap, just like the play before, and I gave the ball to Kevis and ran the opposite direction. I remember locking eyes with the defensive end as I ran his way, and then my attention was diverted with a roar from the sidelines. I looked back in the direction of where Kevis was running, and he had broken free into the secondary! He was flying down the sidelines with a few defenders chasing him. When I saw him out in front headed toward the end zone, I took off. I ran so fast after Kevis that I actually beat almost everyone down the field to meet him in the end zone! Touchdown Reivers!

After Joliet failed to score on their next possession, the ball was punted back to us. Stroh called my first pass play and told me, "Relax. Don't rush. Go through your progressions." I walked up to the line and nonchalantly examined the left side of the field where my intended targets would be. I recognized the cover 3 defense and was anticipating the underneath crossing route being open. I caught the snap and watched the linebacker as he widened and got depth. Bingo! My presnap read was correct, and I was ready to hit the drag route as soon as my receiver got there. I hit the last step of my drop and took one hitch as the route opened up and went to put it right on the numbers of my slot receiver. As I started my follow through to my target, my throwing motion was cut short as I was drilled from my blind side. I'm a right-handed passer, I was reading the defense on the left side of the field, and the defensive end came from the right side. In the world of QBs, this is considered the "casket closed" side. Taking too many hits head-on, with no warning, can end your career prematurely.

I didn't understand how this was possible. The route concept that I waited to open up was one of the quickest routes in our play-book. How did I get hit so fast, and more importantly, *who* hit me that fast? As I got up from the turf, the defensive end who hit was towering over me. He was huge. And just to add insult to injury, he had his jersey tucked up inside his shoulder pads to make sure everyone in the stadium knew he had a set of abs that looked like an ice tray. His intimidation tactic worked, because I was scared. As my lineman were on their way back to the huddle, I kept wondering how in the world he got to me so quick. I definitely didn't want to yell at Keaton Tuttle, my right tackle, but at the same time, this was somewhat of a life-or-death situation.

I decided to put it behind me, and my attention was quickly diverted to the completion I just threw that went for about seven yards. I was feeling confident, and now with a completed pass under my belt, I could finally get rid of my last bit of anxiousness. I looked over to the sideline and got the hand signal for another pass concept. Stroh called a play that he and I both knew I liked. It was a great route concept against a cover 3, and I threw this ball all the time in practice. As we approached the line, I couldn't help but look over at the defensive end who just assaulted me a few seconds ago. I couldn't get him in of my head. I was supposed to be reading the defensive backfield, but instead my mind was fixed on the potential threat. I called my cadence and got the snap, and as I was dropping back to read the free safety, I could feel the immediate pressure coming from my right side. On this passing route, the read was to the middle of the field, so I could actually see the pressure coming from the right side, unlike the play before when I was blindsided.

I knew the route was never going to develop before the monster got to me, so I bailed. I quickly escaped the pocket to my left to avoid a second encounter with the defensive end, and I had a little space to make a play. I looked downfield as I was rolling out of the pocket and didn't see anyone available to throw to. I wasn't the fastest dude on the field by any stretch of the imagination, so I knew I was only a few seconds away from being surrounded by defenders. I decided to keep it and sprint toward our sidelines to try and pick up as many yards as I could. I made it to the sideline about five yards down the field and stepped out-of-bounds just before getting crushed by two pursuing defenders. My pain threshold is comparable to a five-year-old getting his first shot at the doctor, so I did everything I could to avoid getting hit. I picked up the first down, which was awesome, but as I jogged back to the huddle, I was upset. How did this defensive end get to me so quick two plays in a row? It was going to be next to impossible to throw the ball, if Keaton couldn't give me any time.

As I jogged into the huddle, a couple of guys patted me on the butt and told me, "Nice run, bro." I finally felt like I belonged out on the field, doing what I loved. I knelt down in the huddle and scanned my eyes back and forth as I called the next play. It was another pass play, which fortunately was a quick hitch route to the short side of the field, so I didn't have to be concerned about any pressure. What happened directly after breaking the huddle is something I remember more than the majority of the touchdowns I threw that season. Right after breaking the huddle, Keaton Tuttle, my right tackle who was responsible for my last two near-death experiences, stuck around while everyone else jogged to the line of scrimmage. Before shoving his mouthpiece in and heading to the line, he looked me in the eyes and said, "You're gonna have to throw the ball quick, man. I can't block this guy."

You can't block this guy? That's your job! It was one of the most fearful experiences I'd ever had in sports. I walked to the line replaying his comment over and over. This genetically engineered defensive end has the next fifteen minutes to take free shots at me! How was I supposed to concentrate on my progressions or remember all the film I'd watched when all I could think about was my protector informing me that there would be none for the rest of the game? I was shook, knowing that the person who was responsible for protecting me wasn't just failing, but after two plays had mentally given up. How was I supposed to win the game and my potential future starting spot with no protection? Better yet, how was I supposed to make it through the rest of the game and not get hurt without someone protecting me?

*****

If there's one thing I've learned from my six years of coaching, it's that there are a lot of things in the world of sports that young men and women need protection from. As much as we want to look at big strong athletes and assume they're as developed mentally and emotionally as they are physically, it's not true. They're kids in grown-up's bodies. They need guidance, support, affirmation, discipline, and most importantly protection.

As sports become more popular and more money, status, and power get infused into success, the more corrupt it becomes. One thing I've discovered to be so unique about sports is that winning is attached to human performance. Therefore, coaches tend to see athletes as chess pieces. We don't deal with accounts, the stock market, documents, or inflation. We deal with young men and women who are vulnerable and impressionable. I will be the first to admit that I lose sight of that from time to time.

I had an experience where a player on our team was not performing anywhere near the level we needed him to for us to play him. Unfortunately, he was receiving more scholarship money than any of our other players. It was very frustrating for us as coaches, because of the realization of what we could do with his scholarship money. We discussed pulling his scholarship almost weekly. In some ways, it became something that we resented him for, without saying anything, because it felt like we were wasting money. Every mistake he made was magnified by how much money he was costing the program. I was fortunate enough to lead a Bible study with several guys on my team, the women's basketball team, and the volleyball team. We would meet weekly and dig into God's Word, and it was one of the most rewarding things I've ever done. The player in question was there every time, but I rarely heard him talk about anything personal.

One particular night, we broke up into small groups to talk about what people learned from the message, and he opened up about how much being in college and getting a degree meant to him and his family, how even receiving a college degree was almost unthinkable, because of where he came from and the obstacles he had to overcome just to get a degree. I sat there that night absolutely wrecked, thinking about how easy it was for me to discuss his lack of production and wishing he wasn't getting the money that he was. That night, I realized how distorted my mind-set had been, not only to him but also to other players in similar situations. Naturally, all of this was taking place as I was writing this book, and I realized that this player actually needed protection from *me*!

My obligation as a coach is to protect my players. I was so convicted that night, as I heard him pour out his heart about how much he valued his opportunity to do something that would impact his entire family, and for months, I looked at him like a car with a sticker price that didn't match its worth. I learned that sometimes the people that our players need protection from are the coaches.

Our attitudes, our conduct, our language, and our leadership *will* have lifelong impact on our player's lives. There's nothing that we can do to avoid it. It comes with the power of the position that we carry, and it's important that we use that power to protect our players with all diligence. Is it easy? Absolutely not. There will be situations that come up on a daily basis where our players will need us to protect them, whether they know it's happening or not. Domestic abuse, a shoulder to cry on, a safe place to share personal issues, choosing not to use your players as bargaining pieces, or discerning what information they should be privileged to—the list is endless. We must show up to work each day with a mind-set of how to protect each player on our team. And that doesn't mean that each player will require the same tactic to accomplish this. Every person is different, with a unique background, history, and emotional needs that need to be protected.

When I stood behind the line of scrimmage that Saturday afternoon, I wasn't able to focus. I wasn't able to enjoy the intensity of the game. I wasn't even able to do my job very well, because the thing that was in the back of my mind was that I wasn't protected. Maybe Keaton was doing everything he could to block the defensive end that day, but the message that he relayed came across that he had tried and failed and there was nothing he could do. I was saddled with the responsibility of throwing the ball quicker than I was able to, because I wasn't going to be protected. The lesson that I think can be taken from this is regardless of how many times you fail to protect your players from life, the real world, or even yourself, don't ever give up. Don't ever get to a point where you mentally quit trying to protect your team from things that are in your control. Stand your ground, get back up, and sacrifice what you need to so they can be protected.

What I hope you learn from my story as a coach is to remove the pressure of performance-based acceptance. It's so easy to lose sight of our players as people going through a life that presents daily challenges that they are fighting to overcome. We have a tendency to see them as their free throw percentage or their missed box outs or their weak left hand. When we view them through the lens of their performance, we are guaranteed to miss the things that they need to be protected from.

*****

The Bible says in 1 Peter 5:8, "Stay alert! Watch out for your great enemy, the devil. He prowls around like a roaring lion, looking for someone to devour." It's easy to forget that we have an enemy that hates us and wants to see our lives be destroyed. I felt like I had a roaring lion across from me on the field that day, and I was in dire need of some protection. The Bible tells us that there are two ways that we can find protection—one of the areas we briefly touched on in the last chapter.

> Finally, be strong in the Lord and in his mighty power. Put on the full armor of God, so that you can take your stand against the devil's schemes. For our struggle is not against flesh and blood, but against the rulers, against the authorities, against the powers of this dark world and against the spiritual forces of evil in the heavenly realms. Therefore, put on the full armor of God, so that when the day of evil comes, you may be able to stand your ground, and after you have done everything, to stand. Stand firm then, with the belt of truth buckled around your waist, with the breastplate of righteousness in place, and with

> your feet fitted with the readiness that comes
> from the gospel of peace. In addition to all this,
> take up the shield of faith, with which you can
> extinguish all the flaming arrows of the evil one.
> Take the helmet of salvation and the sword of
> the Spirit, which is the word of God. (Ephesians
> 6:10–17, NIV)

God has given us an entire armor to put on so that we can withstand the attacks of the devil.

Before we can protect and cover our players, we first need to learn how to daily put on our own armor. We talked last chapter about needing to be firmly grounded in the *truth* of God's Word and not let the changes in culture, popular opinion, or facts persuade us away from God's truth.

The next part of the armor is considered the breastplate. This is meant to protect your heart and your vital organs. The Bible tells us to put on *righteousness*. Righteousness means to live morally in right standing with God's rules. The breastplate is such a valuable part of the armor, because what it protects is valuable to human life. One of the reasons so many people are heartbroken, sick, and suffering is because they haven't chosen to live righteously. It's very easy to convince ourselves that our situation is a mess because of other people. It's important that we look in the mirror and truly ask ourselves if we are striving to be holy in our hearts.

The next piece of armor Paul talks about are shoes of *peace that come from the gospel*. At first, it doesn't make sense that shoes would be a part of battle armor. But back when this was written, people didn't have retro Jordans or the new KDs to choose from. They wore sandals—sandals that weren't designed in a laboratory by engineers who work for Nike. It was vital that you had shoes that were reliable and able to withstand miles of walking without falling apart. Most athletes have experienced a time during their career when they had to play in shoes that weren't broke in or didn't fit right. It's almost impossible to play well when your feet hurt and your shoes create blisters. In the same way, our battle against our enemy will be a long and treacherous one, if we don't have the peace that comes from truly knowing and believing the good news of the gospel. We must have that foundation fastened tightly around our feet so that wherever God takes us in life, we are equipped to be protected. Peace comes from knowing the good news of the gospel.

Verse 16 says, in addition to all these things, we are to hold up the shield of *faith*. A shield is critical in war to protect against arrows, guns, and anything else that can be shot at us. The rest of the verse says that the devil sends fiery arrows at us. It's amazing to me that people think the Bible is a boring book! The question is, what are these arrows that Satan throws at us? I think the answer is found in what our shield is made out of—*faith*. The things that Satan throws in our path day in and day out are always intended to hinder our faith. What some Christians don't understand, or know, is that Satan is well versed on the Word of God. In Luke 4, when he tempted Jesus, he used scripture to trip him up. Satan will try to create confusion on a daily basis, and if we don't know exactly what the Word says, we give him a foothold to deceive us. Satan knows that it is by our faith that we are saved, by the blood of Jesus Christ, and he knows that without faith, it is impossible to please God (Ephesians 2:8–9 and Hebrews 11:6). Our faith is what Satan wants to destroy, because if he can ruin our faith, he can separate us from God's will for our lives. So Satan will throw fiery arrows of thoughts, sickness, anger, jealously, and more at us to see if we will take the bait. When life starts to fall apart, and it seems like we have too much on our plate to handle, that is when we must hold up our shield of faith and put our trust in the Lord. Our faith protects us from the devil's fiery arrows.

The Word says next to put on the helmet of *salvation*. After talking about how Satan uses thoughts to distract us, it becomes clearer as to why salvation is meant to protect our head. When a person has a personal relationship with Jesus Christ, and they are saved by the gift of salvation, they are a new creation in Jesus Christ. The old person that they used to be is gone, and the new life in Jesus is now their identity (2 Corinthians 5:17). I think it's easy to confuse salvation with behavior modification. When I hear some people talk about being saved, it sounds more like getting a new paint job on an old beat-up station wagon. It couldn't be further from the truth! When a person receives the free gift of a new life in Christ, they die to their old self, and the spirit inside of them becomes brand new. Our bodies might look the same, but internally we are not the same. This is why Christians use the expression "born again." A person dies to their sinful nature, and they are regenerated with the spirit of the Living God inside of them.

The problem is even though our spirit has been renewed in Jesus, our mind and our bodies didn't get the memo. The life of a Christ-follower is working to get our mind and our body to line up with what has been done in our spirit (Romans 7:7–25). Therefore, we put on the helmet of salvation daily to let the truth of our new life begin to transform our thoughts. The old mind-set we used to have, before knowing Christ, needs to be washed with God's Word so that we can see clearly the good and perfect will that He has for us (Romans 12:2). The way to protect our minds from the thoughts thrown at us is by protecting it with the truth of our salvation.

The last element of the armor of God is the *sword of the spirit.* One area of Christianity that a *Sweet Sixteen* coach must grab ahold of is that the life of a Christ-follower is *not* timid. We have the living spirit of the Creator of the universe inside of us, and we are not called to live a life constantly on defense. Too often I see the church metaphorically bar up their doors and hope the world doesn't sneak inside and corrupt them. 2 Timothy 1:7 says, "For God has not given us a spirit of timidity, but of power, love, and self-discipline." For whatever reason, we aren't reminded enough that we are powerful—designed and created by God to live an abundantly prosperous life. When Jesus created mankind, he said we would have dominion. I know that's not a word we use too often, but dominion means sovereignty or control (Genesis 1:26–28). This understanding of power can only come from developing a relationship with the Holy Spirit that lives within us after accepting salvation.

Satan has been thoroughly and completely defeated. When Jesus died on the cross, over two thousand years ago, and rose again, He defeated death, hell, and the grave and we can live in that victory every day through the Holy Spirit. The Holy Spirit is our sword. His guidance is our weapon, and learning to hear His voice is how we fight.

*****

I understand that for most coaches, it's not appropriate to share your faith with your athletes, but there's no laws against praying for them. As *Sweet Sixteen* coaches, we should pray for the protection of our athletes on a daily basis, physically, mentally, emotionally, spiritually, and sexually. There may be opportunities throughout your time as a coach that you have chances to share your faith with them. I would encourage you to be prepared with a ready answer for them if and when they ask. If you equip yourself with these six pieces of armor daily, you will have the wisdom necessary to know what to say and when to say it.

The second way that God has protected us is with Himself. God doesn't put the responsibility solely on us to protect ourselves; He stands in the gap and protects us. 2 Thessalonians says, "But the Lord is faithful; he will strengthen you and guard you from the evil one." God gives you His promise that not only will He protect you from the schemes of the devil, but also He is faithful in doing so. We live in a world with people who are going to inevitably let us down. As much as your parents, your spouse, your children, and your closest friends love you, they are eventually going to let you down. It's part of being human. But there is a God in heaven who will show up day after day and faithfully protect us! *Sweet Sixteen* coaches have a remarkable opportunity to show the love of God to their team by always protecting.

> So be strong and courageous! Do not be afraid and do not panic before them. For the LORD your God will personally go ahead of you. He will neither fail you nor abandon you. (Deuteronomy 31:6, NIV)

Don't be afraid, for I am with you. Don't be discouraged, for I am your God. I will strengthen you and help you. I will hold you up with my victorious right hand. (Isaiah 41:10, NIV)

The righteous person faces many troubles, but the LORD comes to the rescue each time. For the LORD protects the bones of the righteous; not one of them is broken! (Psalms 34:19–20, NIV)

God is our refuge and strength, always ready to help in times of trouble. (Psalms 46:1, NIV)

We are pressed on every side by troubles, but we are not crushed. We are perplexed, but not driven to despair. We are hunted down, but never abandoned by God. We get knocked down, but we are not destroyed. Through suffering, our bodies continue to share in the death of Jesus so that the life of Jesus may also be seen in our bodies. (2 Corinthians 4:8–10, NIV)

The LORD is my rock, my fortress, and my savior; my God is my rock, in whom I find protection. He is my shield, the power that saves me, and my place of safety. He is my refuge, my savior, the one who saves me from violence. I called on the LORD, who is worthy of praise, and he saved me from my enemies. (2 Samuel 22:3–4, NLT)

Chapter 13

Always Trusts

Growing up, I heard a phrase said from almost every adult that I knew, "Trust is earned, not given." Typically, I would be reminded of this directly after doing something untrustworthy or asking permission to do something that was declined. Trust is such a delicate thing, because it takes such a long time to build and can be destroyed in an instant. When I was younger, I remember being at school and deciding to setting up a long row of dominos. It was for recess, or something like that, and I spent the entire time making a cool design. After spending all that time making this elaborate design, it was the moment to watch the masterpiece that I had created come tumbling down. Naturally, I had to call the teacher and everyone around me over to "ooh" and "ah" at my creation for the grand finale. Once the audience was in place, I tipped over the first domino, sat back, and watched the chain reaction wipe out forty minutes hard work. I got the reaction I had hoped for, and my teacher even clapped for me, but then everyone went back to what they were doing. Meanwhile, I was left there, by myself, with this mess to clean up. I remember thinking that day, *I will never do that ever again. It wasn't worth it.*

Trust is very similar to the dominos that lay on the table and the carpet of my elementary school classroom that day. It takes a long time to build, and it can be wrecked in a moment. I could have built the design at home so I didn't have to knock it down at the end of class, and that way, I could have made it much longer. I could have spent weeks, instead of minutes, building and constructing a beautiful design, but if I still made the decision to tip over the first domino, the result would have remained the same. This is true when it comes to trust. To have a stronger bond of trust, it is going to take more time. You don't build the trust of two best friends, who grew up across the street from each other, the first week of meeting someone your freshman year of high school. Trust takes time to build. Another similarity to dominos is that regardless of how strong trust is, it can be destroyed by one decision. Trust is such a fragile thing, and it must be handled delicately. The last comparison, and maybe the most important, is that just like dominos that have just been knocked over, you can *always* rebuild. Trust can be abused in a moment of selfish or unwise decision-making, but the pieces can always be put back together. The thing that is easy to forget is that the process might have to start all the way at the beginning, and it will take time.

"Trust is earned, not given." Do we really act this way in relationships? I don't think so. As a society, I think we are too quick to put our unwavering trust in people that have not earned it yet. The willingness to meet someone who is essentially a complete stranger and trust them with our heart, our emotions, our secrets, our bodies, and our belongings is shocking. I see people get hurt all the time trusting someone with very serious and personal information that I don't believe they had any business sharing in the first place. The reason why is because people need to be qualified before they can be trusted.

Now, that doesn't sound like a very "Christian" thing to say, does it? Aren't Christians supposed to love everyone? Absolutely, they are. But that doesn't mean you have to blindly trust anyone. These are the lines that get blurred, and I think it's in the gap between love and trust that people get hurt the deepest. In this chapter, we are going to look at the example of Jesus and see how he was able to love everyone, but only trust a few people.

This is another concept that I learned from Apostle Ron Carpenter of Redemption Church. I want to look at John 15, where

Jesus is having a conversation with his disciples. At this point, the disciples had been following Jesus for roughly two years. They left everything they had and chose to follow Him.

> I have loved you even as the Father has loved me. Remain in my love. When you obey my commandments, you remain in my love, just as I obey my Father's commandments and remain in his love. I have told you these things so that you will be filled with my joy. Yes, your joy will overflow! This is my commandment: Love each other in the same way I have loved you. There is no greater love than to lay down one's life for one's friends. You are my friends if you do what I command. I no longer call you slaves, because a master doesn't confide in his slaves. Now you are my friends, since I have told you everything the Father told me. You didn't choose me. I chose you. I appointed you to go and produce lasting fruit, so that the Father will give you whatever you ask for, using my name. This is my command: Love each other.

Jesus starts off by explaining the comparison of God's love for him and His love for His disciples. He tells them the way that they can continue to love Him and His Father is by following His instructions, just as He follows His Father's instructions. He then charges them to love one another and that there is no greater way to do that than to lay down their own life for one another. Throughout the course of the entire Bible, God consistently develops this pattern of how He operates heaven, and then He asks us to follow His example.

The next part of this conversation is what I found so interesting, and I think it helps us understand the line between love and trust. In verse 15, He says, "I no longer call you slaves, because a master doesn't confide in his slaves. Now you are my friends, since I have told you everything the Father told me." This is mind-blowing to me. Jesus asked these twelve men to leave everything they know and follow Him, and after *two years* of being with them, He redefines the relationship and begins to tell him intimate information. He tells them that He is going to requalify their relationship, by letting them know information that His Father has told Him. How many of us are willing to share all our private information over the first cup of coffee? After two years of disciplining them, He decided that they were ready to be trusted with important information. He loved them since they started following Him, but didn't trust them until after two years of teaching them.

*****

As coaches, we have a lot of information that we shouldn't share and a lot of information that we should only share with a select number of people. Having the wisdom and discernment to qualify those people will have a direct effect on how many speed bumps we hit in our career. Our team is a part of our circle, and we will discuss how to handle trust among them later. In regard to people that aren't our players, it's important that we are very selective with what we say to people. As high school, college, and professional coaches, we are public figures. We are known around the community, and people love to gossip about well-known people. Saying too much to the wrong people can cause problems that we're not prepared to handle. Let's take a look at how Jesus dealt with big crowds and giving out information.

> Later that same day Jesus left the house and sat beside the lake. A large crowd soon gathered around him, so he got into a boat. Then he sat there and taught as the people stood on the shore. He told many stories in the form of parables, such as this one:
> "Listen! A farmer went out to plant some seeds. As he scattered them across his field, some seeds fell on a footpath, and the birds came and ate them. Other seeds fell on shallow soil with

underlying rock. The seeds sprouted quickly because the soil was shallow. But the plants soon wilted under the hot sun, and since they didn't have deep roots, they died. Other seeds fell among thorns that grew up and choked out the tender plants. Still other seeds fell on fertile soil, and they produced a crop that was thirty, sixty, and even a hundred times as much as had been planted! Anyone with ears to hear should listen and understand." His disciples came and asked him, "Why do you use parables when you talk to the people?"

He replied, "You are permitted to understand the secret of the Kingdom of Heaven, but others are not. To those who listen to my teaching, more understanding will be given, and they will have an abundance of knowledge. But for those who are not listening, even what little understanding they have will be taken away from them. That is why I use these parables, "For they look, but they don't really see. They hear, but they don't really listen or understand." (Matthew 13:1–13, NLT)

Jesus spent time talking to big crowds all the time, and when He did, He always spoke in parables. If you read the rest of Matthew 13, you will see that He told more stories to the groups of people that flocked to Him. Jesus was one of the most polarizing figures of all time, and people gravitated to Him. If there was social media back then, He would have been on your timeline constantly. Thousands of people would travel for miles just to hear Him speak, and when He did, He spoke in code. He wasn't willing to trust just anyone with such profound information.

We would do well as coaches to learn from his wise example. I have learned in my short coaching career that running your mouth about everything you hear, or know, is a surefire way to get yourself in trouble. We need to have clear lines between our circle, and everyone else, and make sure we have boundaries with what information we give out.

With regard to our teams, trust is one of the key components to success in sports. Without trust, winning will be inconsistent. But trust, even among our team, must go through a process. Jesus spent two years teaching his "team" what the life of a Christ-follower was meant to look like, and He was very slow to tell them everything. Even after redefining them as friends, later in the conversation, He told them that there was more He wanted to tell them, but they weren't ready to hear it yet (John 16:12). We must have boundaries with our players, because not everything is appropriate for them to know. It's also important to understand that there is a time and a place to tell your players something. There may be things that the senior captain on your team should know that you shouldn't tell a freshman. All these choices need to be made with careful thought and consideration. My advice is that you can never go wrong with being overly cautious in this area.

It's also important to understand that among your players, you will more than likely have some players that become a part of your inner circle. This isn't something to avoid, and it's not something that is inappropriate. Because trust is built over time, you are naturally going to have players on your team that you've had more time to grow with than others. This is going to create a stronger foundation of trust with select players on your team. I believe this is why there are captains on a team. Jesus even had his "captains."

Peter, James, and John were Jesus's captains. They saw more miracles than the other disciples, they were the only three Jesus pulled aside at the garden of Gethsemane, and they were the only three Jesus took up the mountain during the transfiguration. There are probably dozens of theological debates as to why Jesus chose these three, but the fact of the matter is He chose them. I think it's valuable to have an inner circle of players, because they bridge the gap between you and the rest of your team. That doesn't mean you give them unlimited access to anything and everything, but some great things can happen when you select a small number of your players to be in your inner circle. This should be well-thought-out, and there needs to be a solid foundation of trust already built between you and the players you select.

Your players have to learn to trust one another as well. Just like with the domino example, trust comes from daily repetition of building that trust. It is not going to happen just because it's important. It takes intentionality and practice. Going back to John 15, Jesus tells His disciples that they are to follow His example of following His Father's commandments—"If you keep my commands, you will remain in my love, just as I have kept my Father's commands and remain in his love." As coaches, we can use this example to build trust within our team.

It starts with having clear instructions and strategies that your players can understand and follow. It doesn't matter if it's a simple thing like switching when the offense does a hand off or something complex, like where to be in shrink spots when a ball screen is happening; the players need to fully understand what the strategy is. This requires us as coaches to be great teachers and communicators. One of the reasons why Jesus had such a profound impact was because He was a phenomenal teacher. If our strategies are unclear about what is supposed to happen on the floor, it will be next to impossible for our players to trust one another. After teaching them the strategies, it's critical that we stick to our plan and teach it consistently. Our players need to hear it over and over to believe in it and execute it habitually.

The next part is allowing them to make mistakes as they learn to trust one another. Defensively, the best teams are the ones who do their job consistently and trust their teammates to do their job as well. I can't tell you the number of times I've asked one of my players why they didn't do their job defensively, and the first comment out of their mouth has something to do with not thinking their teammate was going to do their job. There's a lack of trust. When a post player doesn't leave the paint to rotate on baseline penetration, it might be because they reacted slowly, but most of the time, it's because they're more concerned with their man being left open when they help. When your point guard lets his match-up shoot a wide open three point because they closed out short, afraid of getting beat off the dribble, it shows that they don't trust the scouting report that said all that player does is shoot three points. It shows a lack of trust. And just like relationships, trust takes time to build. As a coach, you *must* put your players in situations on a daily basis where they are required to trust one another. It not only takes time to develop trust, but it takes seeing the strategies actually work for players to begin to believe in and commit to it.

Giving your players opportunities to build trust with one another will begin to stack those dominos. The mistake that coaches make is they don't give their players enough practice trusting one another, and when the pressures of a game start to mount, it wipes out the dominos. Coaches tend to get frustrated when their team doesn't trust one another in a particular area, and so they move on out of frustration. If the lack of trust doesn't get fixed and built up to be strong in practice, that area of the game will collapse under the bright lights.

*****

At the beginning, we talked about how trust is something that can always be built and rebuilt. This is the part that I believe 1 Corinthians 13 is driving home when it says *love always trusts*. Your players are going to be a big part of your life, whether you want them to be or not. You are going to have a profound impact on their future, and they are going to have an equally profound impact on you. Our players will grow in their understanding of what love looks like during the four years that they are under our leadership. The scary thing is they are going to learn it regardless of whether it's modeled correctly or incorrectly. I think it's somewhat humorous that Jesus "coached" the disciples for three and a half years, and we have about the same amount of time with each one of our players. We can learn so much from Jesus about what our impact of coaching should look like.

A *Sweet Sixteen* coach will dedicate themselves to building and rebuilding trust with their players over the time they are in the role of teacher. It's a commitment, and it's one that we shouldn't take lightly. Trust is a two-way street that will require us to learn not only to trust our players but also to give them reason that they can trust us. I think it's easy to assume that because we are the coach, they should automatically trust us while, at the same time, they need to earn ours.

If we go into our relationship with our players from the understanding that we want to earn their trust, I believe it makes them feel important and draws them to trust us back. This also works the same when it comes to rebuilding trust. We need to anticipate that there will be times during our career that trust is going to be broken with our players. We *are* going to make mistakes. Our players *are* going to screw up. It's a part of being human, and we need to be prepared for when it happens. We need to be quick to ask for forgiveness when we abuse trust and understand that it's our responsibility to *earn* it back. It's unfair to think that we can knock down the dominos and put the responsibility on them to set them back up. We also must be humble enough to give our players the opportunity to do the same. If we are going to have a "three-strike policy" with our players, what are the repercussions when we get to three strikes?

The reason that *love always trusts* is because it sacrifices the fear of being hurt and believes the best for the relationship. Our players need to know that we trust them. There is enough fear, worry, and anxiety that comes with competing in sports already. The pressure that kids put on themselves to be perfect is difficult enough to overcome. If we compound that pressure with a lack of trust in them, they won't have the freedom to compete with passion. It's not just enough to have trust in your players; you need to let them hear it. After a loss, after a bad game, or after a turnover or screwing up a play, kids tend to assume their coach is going to give up on them, that the bar of expectation is going to be lowered, since they're not capable of meeting the current standard. There are few things that will drive a player to compete even harder, with more determination, than knowing that regardless of their past failures, you still trust them.

Trust is a powerful thing. It's powerful because it can be deadly, but it can also produce incredible things. The Bible is filled with God's call for us to trust Him. For a lot of people, trust is something they don't give out easily. They've been hurt and taken advantage of, and they've decided it's better to trust no one and be safe. The flaw in that way of thinking is that they will never experience the purest form of safety. When you allow yourself to trust, and the recipient handles it correctly, it allows a person to experience comfort that produces a confidence found nowhere else in life. This is why marriage is so powerful, because a person makes a commitment to trust another human being with the rest of their life, with no guarantee that the recipient won't decide to leave. But when we see a good marriage, or experience it ourselves, we experience something that no other relationship can compare to. Ephesians 5:25 says, "Husbands, love your wives, just as Christ loved the church and gave himself up for her." The Bible tells us that the church is the bride and Jesus is the bridegroom. Christ is calling us to put our trust in Him, because He loves us and will not take advantage of our trust. Before we can work on trusting the people in our lives, we need to trust God.

> But blessed is the one who trusts in the LORD, whose confidence is in him. They will be like a tree planted by the water that sends out its roots by the stream. It does not fear when heat comes; its leaves are always green. It has no worries in a year of drought and never fails to bear fruit. (Jeremiah 17:7–8, NIV)
>
> Trust in the LORD with all your heart and lean not on your own understanding; in all your ways submit to him, and he will make your paths straight. (Proverbs 3:5–6, NIV)
>
> Let the morning bring me word of your unfailing love, for I have put my trust in you. Show me the way I should go, for to you I entrust my life. (Psalms 143:8, NIV)
>
> This is the confidence we have in approaching God: that if we ask anything according to his will, he hears us. (1 John 5:14, NIV)
>
> He will not let your foot slip—he who watches over you will not slumber. (Psalms 121:3, NIV)

Chapter 14

Always Hopes

I believe hope is one of the most sought-after things in the world. People can live without a lot of things, but hope is not one of them. Without hope, we have nothing to look forward to. Without hope, each day seems like a replay of yesterday. Without hope, living loses its purpose.

According to suicide.org (CenterforDiscovery.com),
- every hundred minutes a teen takes their own life,
- suicide is the third leading cause of death for young people age fifteen to twenty-four,
- about twenty percent of all teens experience depression before they reach adulthood,
- only thirty percent of depressed teens are being treated for it, and
- female teens develop depression twice as often as men.

We are in a time in America where our kids aren't just suffering with depression and anxiety—they are taking their own lives to escape the stress that they're dealing with. I believe one of the reasons we have seen such an increase in anxiety, stress, and depression is because kids are not growing up with hope. The pressures of social media, cyberbullying, kids having access to see or say anything they want online, and a decreasing percentage of a biological mother and father in the household are killing our kids.

These same kids are coming into our programs. They are arriving with a suitcase full of fears and worries that most of us didn't have when we were their age. It is so important that we are aware of this reality, and we also provide hope to every person on our team.

Coaches as a whole might be some of the most pessimistic people I know. The majority of the conversations that I am a part of with coaches seem to turn toward the negative at some point. Talking about positive or encouraging things might happen from time to time, but the moment someone brings up a complaint, everyone wants to jump in and bear their burdens. It's like a forest fire. As soon as someone lights the first branch, it spreads faster than you can imagine.

I was having a conversation with a coach not too long ago, and his team was one game away from being crowned conference champions. They had an incredible year and had multiple guys who were going to receive all-conference and potential national recognition. I started the conversation by congratulating him and telling him what a great year they've had, and I'm sure he's been really pleased with how his guys have competed. His response started and ended with how frustrated he was with his team. He said they were inconsistent, lazy, and on any given night could lose to anybody. He didn't say one positive thing the whole conversation. I'm not sure he even said "thank you" before going into his rant. Why do we do this as coaches? Why can't we say anything good about our team without feeling like we're arrogant or setting ourselves up for a mighty fall?

> Finally, brothers and sisters, whatever is true,
> whatever is noble, whatever is right, whatever is
> pure, whatever is lovely, whatever is admirable—
> if anything is excellent or praiseworthy—think
> about such things. (Philippians 4:8, NIV)

If anything is excellent or praiseworthy, think on such things. I could spend the rest of my coaching life just trying to accomplish that one sentence, and I would probably fall short when it's all said and done. The reason that coaches are so negative, and the reason our youth are fighting mental health issues, is due to a common problem. We aren't thinking on the right things. When kids spend six hours a day on social media and see the horrible things that are considered casual to us now, that's all they can think about. When coaches sit in the office together, watch the film of the previous game, and can only comment on all the mistakes that they see, it impossible for them to think about the areas that the team is improving.

The question then becomes, where do we find our hope? If we can't answer that question, then all the feelings and decisions we make will always leave us frustrated and wondering why we are the way we are. Is your hope in your job? What about your salary? Is your hope in your popularity or status? Is it in your winning percentage? Maybe it's in your marriage or your kids? I would encourage you to spend some serious time figuring out, when all the chips are on the table, and you look at your life, what do you put your hope in?

To a lot of people, hope is just wishful thinking. It's what a person has when they're holding onto a Powerball ticket, as the numbers are being read on the TV screen. However, to Christ-followers, hope has a much more concrete meaning. If your hope is in anything temporary, there's always a chance for it to be taken away from you. As much as we don't like to think about that possibility, our money, cars, fame, house, and even our family can be taken away from us at any time. That's why they are not wise things to put our hope in. We can love all the blessings that we have in this life, but our foundation of hope needs to be in something we can rely on.

Hope for a Christian is centered on the promises of God, given to us by His Son and His Word. If I were to get on the Internet right now and purchase a MacBook for my wife, after I put in my information and confirmed the payment, I would receive a confirmation e-mail. If I showed my wife the confirmation e-mail, she would be ecstatic! She would tell me thank you and hug me out of appreciation for the wonderful gift that I gave her. The thing is while she was showing me her gratitude, she would have the same number of laptops that she had before I confirmed the payment, zero. She wouldn't be thanking me because she was holding her new laptop.

She wouldn't be hugging me while her new computer was being set up. She would be excited because of the *hope* she now has in what the e-mail confirms. That e-mail confirms the price has been paid for the laptop and its delivery to our house inevitable.

The question is, why wouldn't she have the same reaction about becoming a millionaire if I came home with a Powerball ticket that I just purchased at the gas station? Because there's no guarantee that I would win the Powerball. The problem with putting our hope in anything of this world is that there's no guarantee that it will work out the way that we hope. There's no guarantee that the company that we work for won't be dissolved and we could find ourselves unemployed. There's no guarantee that we will win a conference championship in the next five years and get a contract extension. There's no guarantee that our son or daughter will be good enough to get a college scholarship. There's no guarantee that all the good deeds we do in our life will make us worthy of an eternity in heaven. All these things leave us wishing for the best outcome, not having anything to rely on.

The reason the blood of Jesus gives Christians such a powerful confidence is the same reason the confirmation e-mail would compel my wife to thank me before getting her laptop. Even though she has not obtained her gift, the e-mail stating the price, the form of payment, the type of laptop that was purchased, and the details of the sale would give Jennifer the hope that all she has to do now is wait. The Bible is our e-mail confirmation that the price of our salvation was the blood of a perfect sacrifice, the form of payment was the Son of God, the type of gift was an eternity in paradise, and the details of the sale are all throughout the sixty-six books.

The problem that some people have with this hope is that we cannot see heaven. To us on earth, it's just an idea that's described in a book. Without a guarantee that heaven exists, it's just wishful thinking that there is a life after this one. But Jennifer wouldn't be able to see her laptop either. She would only be able to rely on a picture of the gift until it arrived. She would have no guarantee that it wasn't an Internet scam trying to steal money from me. Most likely, she would trust that the e-mail is true, because of the reliability that Apple has established. Christians are given the Bible to give us a picture of what heaven will be like when it arrives. This is the confidence of a Christian who puts their hope in Jesus; we trust the Word of God because of the reliability it has shown us, by changing us from the inside out after believing in Him.

The power of this hope is that it makes all the ups and downs of this life become less overwhelming. Everything that we go through and endure in this life is merely a part of the five to seven business days that the package takes to ship. The heartbreaking reality is that the majority of the youth in our country, who are struggling with mental health, are in the place they're in because they don't know of the hope of Jesus Christ. The worries of their young lives seem so magnified, because they don't know what else there is to life besides their struggles. The reason why coaches constantly agonize over their team's deficiencies is because their hope is in how many championships they can win, and each game that they lose is one step closer to their hopes being shattered another year.

Where we put our hope in this life determines how we handle every circumstance that we face. And because we are responsible for the well-being of our players, that means we need to set the example of what putting your hope in something reliable looks like.

*****

When it comes to what happens on the court, *Sweet Sixteen* coaches need to create an environment of hope to help their team compete. A team that plays without hope will never compete with the same tenacity as one who does. In 2015, I was a volunteer assistant coach at Des Moines Area Community College. We had a strong group of returning sophomores who made the NJCAA National Tournament the year before. Our expectation going into the season was to get back to the tournament and at least make it to the Final Four. The interesting thing about the format for the national tournament is that it's a double-elimination-style tournament. The teams who get beat in one of the first two rounds of the tournament have to come back and compete for, at best, seventh-place finish in the consolation bracket.

We were fortunate to win our first game in the tournament and had a day off before we would play in the Sweet Sixteen. The coaching staff went over to the arena in Danville, Illinois, to watch the team we would play on Thursday, and we saw a few consolation games while we were there. Watching the consolation games between the teams who had already lost a game and had no chance of winning the national championship showed what hopeless basketball looks like. These games were horrible. Several of the teams played sloppy from start to finish. The bench players weren't engaged in the game. The head coaches were constantly trying to coach effort, and the players were all playing incredibly selfish.

How could a team who two days ago was locked in, fired up, and competing with everything they had look like a completely different team less than twenty-four hours later? They were at the national tournament! The one key element that had been taken away from them was hope. Those teams showed up that week in March with one goal in mind—win the national championship. When the thing that had given them hope was stripped from them, their willingness to compete with the same desire was gone.

I learned something from watching those consolation games that day, and later that week, I would experience it firsthand. We won our first three games and were headed to the Final Four! Not only did we get to the Final Four, like we had set out to do at the beginning of the season, but also we were matched up against John Wood Community College, who we had beat twice during the regular season. They were a talented team that was well coached, but we were the more talented team. The game was incredibly competitive, and unfortunately, they went on a big run late in the second half, pulled away, and ended our hopes of a national championship.

We had to come back the next day and play for the third and fourth place. Our guys were devastated after the loss to John Wood, and it showed the following day. The same lack of emotion, disinterest, and selfishness that I saw the second day of the tournament was now happening within our team. As we went through the motions for forty long minutes, we got down to a very good Phoenix College team and stayed down the entire game. It was one of the most disappointing games I've ever been a part of. There was nothing we could say, no play we could draw up, and no substitutions we could make to bring our team back from the grave. They were mentally and emotionally hopeless. Without the potential to hoist the national championship trophy, our team didn't have the desire to compete.

Something that I would encourage you to do with your team is to have multiple goals that your team can achieve throughout the season. It's easy to make a goal of winning a conference championship or getting to the Elite Eight or winning a national championship, and I would never discourage anyone from making that their goal. However, if the goals that are put in front of a team to achieve become unattainable, the same thing that happened to our team at DMACC will happen to yours. In sports, players always need to have a goal in front of them to put their hope in. For a starter, it could be making the postseason tournament. For a walk-on/bench player, it could be getting minutes in the game. For an injured player, it could be a timeline of getting back to full-contact practice. For a role player, it might be improving two or three of their statistical categories from the previous season. No matter what the goals are that are put in front of your players, there needs to be something they're working toward. Without the potential to achieve, hope is lost.

It is critical that you take time before each and every season to think about the hope that you want to create for the year. This shouldn't be something that is a routine or gets repetitive. Be creative and thoughtful about each individual and the potential you see for the season. It needs to be realistic, but it also needs to be difficult. There should be goals that can be achieved earlier in the year, midway through the year, and something to strive for down to the last game of the season. This will create opportunities for your team to either see success early and be motivated to keep pushing or deal with a small amount of failure and be driven to finish strong. Nobody knows your team better than you, so you're the most qualified person to set the vision for your program. Take time to create goals both individually and for the team. Maybe sit down with them and have them come up with some on their own. It's good for players to have personal achievements that they are working toward while also seeing how those goals can be met while making the team goals the main priority. If there is always the element of hope present on a daily basis, you will get the most out of your players.

*****

We need to remember that life is about more than basketball. As much as we grind day in and day out to win games and bring home championships, basketball is not the most important thing in life. Our players are going to stop playing at some point, and when they're done, they need to find purpose in life outside of sports. One thing I see happen to professional athletes is they don't have hope outside of their athletic career. Their identity, their purpose, and their joy are all wrapped up in the success they achieve in sports. Like we talked about earlier, sports are a temporary pleasure in life. MJ stopped bouncing the ball eventually. Wayne Gretzky had to take the skates off at some point. Tom Brady won't win Super Bowls forever. Tiger Woods might not ever get another major championship. Sports can bring us a ton of happiness, but it can't be the place we find our hope. It's not a solid foundation no matter how successful you are.

Coaches have such a profound impact on their players, because they get to impart so many life skills into a young person's daily routine. Coaches get to teach their players how to be disciplined, respectful, honest, hardworking, humble, selfless, and much more. These are things that will last much longer than trophies and accolades, but it must be a priority to us, if it's going to be a priority to them. If all we talk about is winning, then all our players will know we care about is winning. We get the wonderful opportunity to encourage our players to think critically and establish faith, hope, and a belief system for the first time being away from home as a young adult. The years, months, days, and moments that you have with your players are *critical!* Make sure you take advantage of the time you have with them, because it will be gone before you know it.

Hope is one of the most profound substances in life. It can't be touched, tasted, or substituted but it gives people a reason to get up in the morning. Life is hard. No matter what family you were born into, how talented you are, what your credit score is, or how many rings you have in a trophy case, life has a way of dealing everyone a few bad hands. It's hope that gives us the courage and the confidence to look every season of life in the face and know that we can get through it. Before you can love your team through the expression of *always hoping*, you first have to know where your hope comes from. Some of you *believe* in Jesus Christ, but you haven't been willing to put your *hope* in Him. Believing in Him is important, but it's not enough. James chapter 2 explains this.

> What good is it, my brothers and sisters, if someone claims to have faith but has no deeds? Can such faith save them? Suppose a brother or a sister is without clothes and daily food. If one of you says to them, "Go in peace; keep warm and well fed," but does nothing about their physical needs, what good is it? In the same way, faith by itself, if it is not accompanied by action, is dead. But someone will say, "You have faith; I have deeds." Show me your faith without deeds, and I will show you my faith by my deeds. You believe that there is one God. Good! Even the demons believe that—and shudder. You foolish person, do you want evidence that faith without deeds is useless? Was not our father Abraham considered righteous for what he did when he offered his son Isaac on the altar? You see that his faith and his actions were working together, and his faith was made complete by what he did. And the scripture was fulfilled that says, "Abraham believed God, and it was credited to him as righteousness," and he was called God's friend. You see that a person is considered righteous by what they do and not by faith alone. (James 2:14–24, NIV)

Even demons believe that there is one God. When I read this for the first time, it changed the way I viewed Christianity and hope.

The Bible is clear that it's not enough to simply believe in God. We must rely on Him, by putting our hope in His promises. Before we can teach our players how to hope, we must be grounded in it ourselves. If you are in a place where you're still not convinced by the truths of God's Word, I would encourage you to do any honest evaluation of where you find your hope. Can it last for a lifetime? Will it endure all the trials and disappointments of life? More importantly, when the breath in your lungs is gone, will your hope still exist after this life? God is calling you to put your trust in the hope that only He can provide. Will you make the commitment to put your hope in Him?

Take some time to really think about what God promises us, His children, about the hope He has freely given us.

> He gives strength to the weary and increases the power of the weak. Even youths grow tired and weary, and young men stumble and fall but those who hope in the LORD will renew their strength. (Isaiah 40:29–31, NIV)

> Being confident of this, that he who began a good work in you will carry it on to completion until the day of Christ Jesus. (Philippians 1:6, NIV)

> "For I know the plans I have for you," declares the LORD, "plans to prosper you and not to harm you, plans to give you hope and a future. Then you will call on me and come and pray to me, and I will listen to you. You will seek me and find me when you seek me with all your heart." (Jeremiah 29:11–13, NIV)

> May the God of hope fill you with all joy and peace as you trust in him, so that you may overflow with hope by the power of the Holy Spirit. (Romans 15:13, NIV)

For in this hope we were saved. But hope that is seen is no hope at all. Who hopes for what they already have? But if we hope for what we do not yet have, we wait for it patiently. (Romans 8:24–25, NIV)

Chapter 15

Always Perseveres

"Tre Jones lays it in, and just like that, the lead is back to fourteen," the announcer said, feeling a shift in the atmosphere of KFC Yum! Center in Louisville, Kentucky, on February 12th. The University of Louisville was taking it to Duke University for thirty-four minutes of an ACC conference matchup in front of a sold-out crowd, all dressed in black. It was the first time the entire year that the freshman phenoms, who could easily be mistaken for the *Space Jam* Monstars, were finally looking like the eighteen-year-olds that they were.

The game had been a blowout almost from the first media time-out. The Cardinals forced Duke to shoot outside the paint early and got ahead by a comfortable lead going into the second half. Duke played a very uncharacteristic second half and looked as though all their powers had been taken from them, when they left the locker room. They couldn't hit a free throw. They couldn't catch a pass. They turned the ball over. Cam Reddish, Tre Jones, and RJ Barrett were as cold as ice from the three-point line; and even though Zion Williamson was on pace to have, yet another twenty and ten night, they were nowhere close to the Cards.

With 10:30 left on the clock, the score was 56-36 in favor of Louisville, and the feeling in the arena was that either it was going to get uglier or they would jog across the finish line with a comfortable lead. Duke had only suffered two losses the entire year, and one of them was to an incredible Gonzaga team during Thanksgiving Break at the Maui Invitational. Since then, they were 16-1 and showed no signs of losing any steam. However, on this particular night, the odds just didn't seem to be in their favor. Everything that could go wrong seemed to, and the players on the court, as well as the coaches on the bench, looked as though a loss was inevitable.

The color commentator summed up Duke's performance with roughly eleven minutes left on the clock when he said, "How about the opinion that a good ol' fashion fanny paddling is good for the soul?" To which his partner replied, "If that's the case, Duke's soul ought to be nice and clean after this one." #2 ranked Duke wasn't just going to get beat tonight; they were going to be embarrassed to the tune of a twenty-point loss.

Then something happened with six minutes and some change left that I don't think I'd ever seen before. Duke went on a 7-0 run around the nine-minute mark that was answered by a corner three from Dwayne Sutton that put the lead back to nineteen points. Zion Williamson came down, drove to the basket, and made a hoop, plus the harm for an and-1 that cut the lead to sixteen. Duke pressed after the free throw and forced a quick turnover in the backcourt that lead to a Tre Jones layup, and Louisville head coach Chris Mack was forced to take a time-out to stop the momentum. What happened next caught my attention.

Duke ran over to the bench with the most serious look of determination in their eyes, as the bench players erupted, going out to congratulate them. Freshman Joey Baker was seen on national TV shouting to his teammates, "Let's go! Right now!" The energy in their huddle was electric. Every player was high-fiving, looking one another in the eyes with the confidence that they were going to win the game, no matter what. It was incredible. I had never seen a team struggle in absolutely every facet of a game, down twenty, and after shaving a few points off the lead look like they were up by thirty! It was a living example of *perseverance*. They had so many opportunities to throw in the towel, sub in their backups, and say, "Well, it just wasn't our night." As a matter of fact, the guard who forced the steal with 6:15 left, by diving on the floor for a loose ball, missed a wide-open fast break layup, with nobody around him, less than two minutes before forcing the steal. I know players who would have been so embarrassed by their mistake that they would have let it affect the rest of the game. Jordan Goldwire moved on like he had short-term memory loss.

In the remaining 6:09 of the second half, Duke forced Louisville to turn the ball over six times while only allowing them to take five shots the rest of the game! In four minutes and fifty seconds, Duke came back from a fourteen-point deficit to tie the game and took the lead with under thirty seconds to play. An arena decked out in 22,000 black T-shirts went from jumping around and cheering to complete silence, as the Blue Devils made one of the most impressive comebacks in school history.

Where did this perseverance come from? What gave them the will power and belief to trust in one another and themselves to come back from what looked to be an insurmountable deficit? As I watched the last six minutes of the game, I wasn't even in the arena, and I could feel the momentum shifting. With each turnover, the crowd grew more silent, and Duke believed a little more that they could come back. With each basket the Blue Devils scored, their ensuing full-court press had a little bit more intensity. As the lead continued to shrink, with every point, the crowd went from excited cheers to an arena absolutely stunned.

In the postgame interview, Zion Williamson was asked what head coach Mike Krzyzewski said to them at the eight-minute media time-out, before they started to make their miraculous comeback. Zion responded, "Coach K just told us, 'I don't coach losers.'" What a message to tell your team while they're down by twenty, with less than ten minutes to play. But Coach K's players believed it. They walked back onto the court having played miserable for thirty-two minutes, hearing the comments from the opponent's fans, feeling the frustration of their poor performance, and believed they weren't losers.

Their strong belief in one another, their leader, and themselves and the hard work they put in daily gave them the mental fortitude to preserver, because deep within themselves, they trusted their coach when he told them, "I don't coach losers." At that moment, losing was no longer an option; it was merely a barrier between them and who their leader told them they were. The trust they had in their head coach was the backup generator to their perseverance. I want to be the type of coach that can grab the hearts of every team I have the opportunity to coach and get them to believe no game is ever lost, until it's over.

*****

How can we reproduce this same perseverance in our programs? I believe the first thing we have to keep in mind is that having a team with great perseverance does *not* mean that you will win every game you play. The culture that we need to strive to create and sustain is a team that no matter what the obstacle, we will never give up. The goal is to have a team that continues to put forth maximum effort regardless of the score and doesn't let adversity affect their trust in one another or themselves.

One key element that is indicative of a team who struggles with perseverance is complaining. Sports create situations on a daily basis where you have to deal with adversity. Things don't go the way you planned, referees make bad calls, buses arrive late to pick you up or drop you off, and the list is a mile long. There's no way to antici-pate the ways your program will face adversity, because it's always something different. There is an expression that says, "Life is ten percent what happens to you and ninety percent how you react to it." This is a direct reflection of perseverance. When things go wrong and circumstances out of your control show up, does your team start to complain? Are they quick to call things unfair or determine that the negative incident won't allow them to be successful? If these are things you've noticed on your team or you find yourself doing, there's a lack of perseverance in your program.

Another way we can identify our team's level of perseverance is how they respond when they're losing. Does your team come together and find confidence in one another, or do they splinter off and become five individuals? We see this happen a lot when teams are losing, and there's a sense of urgency to cut into the lead. Individual players feel the pressure to "take over" and try to bring the team back single-handedly. Once one person comes down and tries to make a heroic play, the other four players are frustrated and think they have the right to do the same thing the next time they get the ball. It becomes contagious, and before the coach can call a time-out, the team has essentially wasted four to five possessions by being selfish. While the offense is ineffective, players stop communicating and giving effort on defense, and before you know it, the eight-point lead is now sixteen. When you notice players on your team trying to make home-run plays every time they touch the ball when your team is struggling, that's a clear sign that perseverance is lacking. There isn't trust in the game plan or a belief that continuing to work as a team will turn the game around.

I believe that perseverance is a learned skill. For our players to learn how to persevere, they *must* but given opportunities to do so, before the stands are full and the scoreboard is turned on. A good coach will intentionally create environments that forces their teams to have to battle some adversity. Playing four on five, restricting the offense from dribbling, and telling one team that they are only allowed to run one specific play are great ways to see how your team reacts to adverse situations. It's crucial to evaluate how each player handles difficult circumstances, as well as how the team as a unit comes together in times of stress. When these intentional situations of adversity are happening during your practices, your toughest players will stand out. At the same time, your mentally weak players will also identify themselves very quickly.

When you're creating these opportunities, it is equally as important to talk about how your players responded individually and as a unit and talk about what went well and what needs to continue to improve. As I said before, perseverance is a learned skill. It has to be practiced and engrained into your team. The book of James refers to this, and I think it does a great job of explaining why adversity is necessary.

> Consider it pure joy, my brothers and sisters, whenever you face trials of many kinds, because

> you know that the testing of your faith produces
> perseverance. Let perseverance finish its work so
> that you may be mature and complete, not lack-
> ing anything. (James 1:2–4, NIV)

This text speaks directly to why it's so valuable for your team to be put in adverse situations. James says that when we are tested, it produces perseverance, and when that perseverance is allowed to finish its work, it will make us mature and complete, not lacking anything. I think of the dozens of games I have watched where a team down the stretch, in a high-pressure game, does some incredibly immature things that cause them to lose the game. The Bible tells us that we need to allow tests to challenge us in our lives so that we can grow in our perseverance for the next test. One of the most disappointing things to see as a coach is a player who makes an immature mistake on the court, and the next time they are put in the same situation, they make the same mistake because they didn't learn from the first failure.

For our team to be mature and complete, not lacking any-thing, we need to show them the value of enduring tests. And a *Sweet Sixteen* coach won't just stop there—they will work to get their team to consider it pure joy when they are being tested. A team that looks at adversity and can find joy in it will always find a way to achieve more than they should. Apply these verses to your daily practices and see how they begin to mature your team.

One of the most powerful examples of perseverance that your team can learn from is when the coach practices what they preach. As the leader of your program, it is your job to teach your players how to persevere when things aren't going well, not only through your instruction but also how you handle adversity yourself. You must be the most mentally tough person in your entire program, because the team will look to you to determine whether victory is achievable. And this isn't just in the words you speak, but it's in the body lan-guage that you give off. Your facial expression, how you cross your arms, the way you sit in your chair, and how you react to things on the court tell the story of what's going on in your mind. Coaches need to be very cognizant of their body language on the sidelines, because it can directly affect the team's ability to persevere.

This same perseverance is a key component in *agape*. We just spent the last eleven chapters talking about these incredibly difficult demands of love. To love our players the way God calls us to is not easy! Perseverance is required in love, because we will struggle on a daily basis to accomplish *agape love*. We will probably experience feelings of inadequacy to successfully master even half of *The Sweet Sixteen*, and we are going to have to rely on perseverance to keep fighting. But where do we find the strength to persevere? Where is our "Coach K moment" that provides us the belief in ourselves that we aren't losers?

> In fact, this is love for God: to keep his commands. And his commands are not burdensome, for everyone born of God overcomes the world. This is the victory that has overcome the world, even our faith. Who is it that overcomes the world? Only the one who believes that Jesus is the Son of God. (1 John 5:3–5, NIV)

The Bible provides us several "Coach K moments" and this is one of them. We can know and believe that in every situation in our lives, we are victorious through Jesus Christ and His sacrifice. The confidence that we need to persevere through the hills and valleys of our lives will always come back to knowing and believing that Jesus Christ conquered the grave! We are sinners who will perpetually fall short, turn back to our bad habits, and find ourselves "on the road and down by twenty with very little time left." We are going to deal with the memories of all the bad choices we've made, just like Duke kept thinking about the turnovers, the missed layups, and the 4-20 shooting performance from the three-point line. But just like Coach K looked them in the eyes and told them you're not losers, our Father in heaven says in His love letter to us that we're not losers either. In fact, He reminds us that we can persevere because we *already* have victory over the world.

Many of you had no idea what love actually looked like before reading this book. I know I have misappropriated love many times, over the course of my life, because I hadn't seen the true picture of God's love. But after studying *The Sweet Sixteen*, I realized we need to be very cautious about using the word "love" so flippantly. Now, after knowing what God's love requires, it seems intimidating to even attempt putting these expectations on yourself. A lifetime of failing, and coming up short seems to be inevitable when love requires such a high demand on our actions. John 8:32 says, "Then you will know the truth, and the truth will set you free." Now that we know the truth of what love really is, described by the Creator of love, the Bible tells us that we can be set free. I don't know about you, but at first glance this whole concept seems more damning than freeing. If you're feeling that way, it could be because you're focusing too much on your abilities, and not enough attention on Christ's victory. Here are some points that we as followers of Christ need to keep at the forefront of our minds;

1. The love of God is the most powerful substance on earth, and having an understanding of it compels us to love others the way Christ first loved us.
2. We, as sinful people, will never love one another in a way that accurately reflects how great our God's love is for His creation.
3. Because of that great love, God forgave us for our inability to meet His standard of love even before we had an opportunity to disappoint Him.
4. The freedom comes through understanding the truth that we will always fall short of His standard, but He extends more grace each time we miss the mark.

What John is saying, is that knowing the truth sets us free to run after love with pure intentions, and it also gives us a clear understanding of whether or not we are making progress. We no longer have to be mentally tied up by the frustration of knowing we have kept every record of wrong done to us for the past five years. We don't have to stop running the race because we struggle with cussing. Freedom says, "On your best day, you fall short of how indescribable God's love is, so don't beat yourself up over your mistakes." While at the same time, He gives us very clear and tangible standards for us to align our conduct up against. The goal is progression, not perfection.

In life, we are going to face obstacles that make us want to give up. We are going to want to take the easy way out, settle for mediocre, and put our effort on cruise control. I have a number of areas in love that I want to sweep under the rug and pretend that growing in other areas nullifies my refusal to work on the hard parts. The messy and beautiful thing about the love God calls us to is that it will require a lifetime commitment. We will never graduate from Love University. This is why one of the final traits of *The Sweet Sixteen* is a willingness to persevere. There is no finish line to this race. And for some people, that can seem cruel and deter them from wanting to even try. If I can't ever master this lifelong goal, why would I put in any effort at all?

That is a logical and reasonable question, but let's compare it to our sport. I don't know of anyone who has never missed a shot in a game. I don't know of any team who has never lost. I can't think of one kicker who is a hundred percent in their career. There are zero QBs who have never thrown an interception. So why do they practice? Why do they spend all that time trying to perfect an imperfectible craft? It's a waste of time, isn't it? (Hopefully you see where I'm going.)

It's the grind, the late hours, the losses, and the monotonous training that make all the victories along the way worth it. Without the sadness of defeat, the victories wouldn't be as rewarding.

I can tell you that the incredible relationships you will get to experience through all the failures will always outweigh the setbacks. Don't let the fear of failure keep you from pursuing excellence. God's Word has the amazing ability to call you to a higher standard in a way that gives us hope and encouragement while also reminding us how much further we still have to go. Our ability to persevere the tough losses of this world can only happen when we know that "God doesn't create losers." Whether you've been abused, molested, raped, bankrupt, incarcerated, depressed, or suicidal, God didn't create you a loser. Those are just a part of your story that God can use to show the world that the worst tests in life still can't destroy what God has put a purpose in.

Under our own strength, persevering can seem impossible. It can be scary, and it can hurt. But through God, we are more than conquers. If you are in a place in life where you are trying to persevere all by yourself, I want to invite you to let God carry your burden for you. Jesus says in Matthew 11:28–30, "Come to me, all you who are weary and burdened, and I will give you rest. Take my yoke upon you and learn from me, for I am gentle and humble in heart, and you will find rest for your souls. For my yoke is easy and my burden is light."

> Blessed is the one who perseveres under trial because, having stood the test, that person will receive the crown of life that the Lord has promised to those who love him. (James 1:12, NIV)

> Stand firm, and you will win life. (Luke 21:19, NIV)

> Therefore, since we have been justified through faith, we have peace with God through our Lord Jesus Christ, through whom we have gained access by faith into this grace in which we now stand. And we boast in the hope of the glory of God. Not only so, but we also glory in our sufferings, because we know that suffering produces perseverance; perseverance, character; and character, hope. And hope does not put us to shame, because God's love has been poured out into our hearts through the Holy Spirit, who has been given to us. (Romans 5:1–5, NIV)

I consider that our present sufferings are not worth comparing with the glory that will be revealed in us. (Romans 8:18, NIV)

We are hard pressed on every side, but not crushed; perplexed, but not in despair; persecuted, but not abandoned; struck down, but not destroyed. (2 Corinthians 4:8–9, NIV)

Peace I leave with you; my peace I give you. I do not give to you as the world gives. Do not let your hearts be troubled and do not be afraid. (John 14:27, NIV)

Chapter 16

Love Never Fails

Failure—it's a word we try to avoid at all costs in our profession. It's what drives coaches to scream, cuss, cheat, belittle, and lose sleep over. Failure is the number one threat that hovers over our lives each and every day as a coach. Even the greatest teams in the history of sports couldn't avoid the mighty clutches of failure. The climax of 1 Corinthians 13 is one of the most challenging yet hope-filled statements you'll find in the scripture. However, in sports, we are going to deal with failure. It's a part of the business that we signed up for. We need to have the maturity and the wisdom to deal with failure in a way that brings hope to our team. The greatest coaches aren't the ones whose teams never lose. They're the ones who grow the most from every setback.

In America, we are incredibly blessed. The resources that we have access to are significantly different in most other parts of the world. I believe that the success of our country has driven us to have an expectation of success in everything we do. Very few people, especially young people, are content simply being average. Everyone wants to be the best at everything, and we want for everyone to perceive us in that light. Social media is a prime example of people constantly trying to portray themselves with their best foot forward.

The American Dream is nothing like it was years ago. The "dream" used to be being able to live free from the government controlling all your decisions while being able to financially support your family doing what you're passionate about. In today's culture of young adults, they want everything *now*. They want to have the same things that their parents spent thirty years working for within six months of being out of college. Athletes want to be the star day one of practice rather than coming in with the mind-set that they are going to work as hard as they can to show the coach over time that they are ready to help the team be successful. I believe it is because of the evolving mind-set of young people that we struggle with the idea of failure. If I ask my mother or my grandparents what their impression of failure is, more than likely, they are going to say that it's simply a part of growing. If I were to ask a millennial the same question, I'm probably going to get an answer that speaks to how they try to avoid it at all costs.

There's a common phrase in athletics that says, "Sports don't build character. Sports reveal character." I believe that sports are able to do both. Sports teach so many wonderful lessons that ultimately will continue to show up in different forms throughout the life of a person. Learning how to deal with disappointment, difficult tasks, leadership, being on time, working together with a team, and discipline are all things that are very much a part of life after sports. If we give ourselves, as coaches, to diligently teaching those skills to our players, we can set them up to carry those characteristics into their adult life.

On the other hand, we also see where a person's character is at through sports. All of those qualities that I said we can help teach our players to value are areas that we will be able to evaluate very quickly due to the nature of sports. A common thread through this entire book is that our players are always going to come into our programs with a number of bad habits, mind-sets, and deficiencies based on their upbringing. This is what the expression means when it says, "Sports reveal character." We will see all the good and bad traits in our players as we grow with them through our sports, but we need to identify the character of our players while building it at the same time. If you simply think it's one way or the other, then either you will be blind to their current flaws or you will assume there's nothing you can do to help them grow.

We *must* teach our team how to deal with failure. I believe that more value is gained through handling failure in a mature way and learning to better yourself from it than a lot of victories. Winning has a way of hiding a lot of problems. When you suffer a loss, it's the most important time for you to be the best coach you can be in that moment, because it's in that moment that players start to question themselves, their teammates, and possibly even you. It's also in those moments that people are most receptive to correction when it's done in the right way. There's nothing like the feeling of failure to open you up to criticism, because people don't want to experience that pain again! It's imperative that we find the courage to meet failures head on and be the best version of ourselves in moments of defeat. We can build character in our players that will be with them the rest of their lives, if we can love them through failure.

The purpose of this book is less about winning games and more about winning the hearts of your players. Being successful and winning championships will bring you a remarkable amount of happiness, but pure joy will only come from the bond that is created with the people in your life. That is why we are finishing with the most powerful charge of all—*love never fails*.

You are going to go through the best of times and the worst of times over your coaching career. The most unthinkable victories and the heart-shattering losses are going to be painted on the canvas of your professional career. My heart's desire is that *The Sweet Sixteen* will equip you to meet every experience with love. Sports are exciting because we can never accurately predict the outcome. The Cinderella stories, the comebacks, and the upsets are the thrill of sports. And life is going to bring us all of the same exciting thrills. As we navigate through all these experiences, we are left with the hope that love will never fail. I think this means two things for us.

First, it means that we can find rest in knowing that if we are willing to write these traits on the tablets of our hearts and give our career to pursuing these things, we will never fail. There's a promise made by God that even when we find ourselves losing the battle, love will always win out. That is the confidence we can have as we begin or continue this journey.

The second meaning is that we don't get to quit. There are numerous things in my life that I was so dedicated to at the start. I planned for it, I told people about my new commitment, I wrote it down, and I did many other things to fire myself up. Then when it got difficult, I stopped seeing progress, or the passion died out, I quit. *Agape* doesn't come with a cancellation agreement. It's not a diet, or a fad, or a wagon that you can fall on and off. Either you're in or you're out when it comes to *agape*. For those of you who have been convicted throughout this book about telling your players you love them and not backing it up with your actions, this is for you. You have to make the choice to be all in or all out. This doesn't mean you're committing to not making mistakes or falling short. It means that you're making a commitment to pursue love and never wave the white flag.

Some of your players have never experienced love in their life. They've never had someone be patient when they struggle or show them kindness when they don't deserve it or didn't use them for personal gain. Some of you have no idea how amazing one of your players could end up becoming if someone would love them for the first time. The thing about love is that when it's given unconditionally, it pulls something out of the receiver that nothing else in life can do. It awakens things inside of a soul that remain dormant until love brings it to life. You have been blessed with a job that gives you an opportunity to do this every time you step on the court.

It's no secret that there are some people that are simply easier to love than others. You are going to have your "favorites" as you walk through your coaching career, and I think that's very normal. Some of your players are going to be very difficult to love. There are kids who grow up in environments or circumstances that leave them with dozens of unseen scars. They are going to come into your program with loads of baggage that not even Southwest Airlines would let fly for free. As much as we don't want to hear this, those are the very players that we need to love the most. God designed each one of us with the capacity to love and the desire to be loved by others. There are young people who have never been given the opportunity to experience both of those, and it damages them. It makes them closed off, defiant, and disrespectful. The only cure for a damaged soul is the power of *agape*.

If we are going to make a commitment to love, we need to love hard! Don't hold anything back. It's no different than the way we urge our players to compete. "Give 110%," "Run through a wall for your teammates," "Don't leave anything left on the court"—these are all things we try to pull out of our players, because we know that's how success is achieved, through giving your whole heart to it. God is calling us to do the same, when we commit to loving our players. I'll be the first to tell you that it is the ultimate sacrifice to take the challenge of a *Sweet Sixteen* coach. But I can tell you from personal experience that I have yet to experience a win in my entire coaching career that can measure up to giving my heart to my players and loving them with the powerful love of God.

This book has a great deal of information in it. The amount of scripture, teaching, and examples would need to be read over and over to retain all of it. The amazing thing is I barely scratched the surface of all that God's Word has to say on the matter. And as much as this book is catered to coaches learning how to love their players, it's actually more about you.

Every scripture in this book is for your benefit, to help you grow into the best coach you could ever be. Don't get me wrong, strategy, game planning, X's and O's, and what plays to run are extremely important. But thirty years from now, you'd be lucky if a handful of people ever remember any of those things. If you want to leave your thumbprint on the hearts of your players, if you want the lessons you taught your teams to be passed down to their children and their children's children, then it starts with you allowing God to be your *Sweet Sixteen* coach.

We've talked ad nauseam about love. We have looked at every trait that represents it and exposed the areas that coaching has abused this powerful creation and hurt people along the way. What you need to know about love is that God didn't just create us with the potential to give and receive love. God is love. You cannot separate the two. God isn't just a great example of what we should model ourselves after; love is His DNA. When we read through 1 Corinthians 4:13, we can put God in the place of love.

> God is patient, God is kind. God does not even, He does not boast, He is not proud. He does not dishonor others, He is not self-seeking, He is not easily angered, He keeps no record of wrongs. God does not delight in evil but rejoices with the truth. God always protects, always trust, always hopes, always perseveres. God never fails.

Some of you need to know that God loves you. He loves you right where you are in your brokenness and in your incredibly successful life. You were designed by the Creator of the universe with a God-shaped hole in your heart that only He can fill. He loves you more than you could know, and His desire is to have a real, authentic relationship with you!

To be a *Sweet Sixteen* coach, you have to first experience the love of your heavenly Father before you can give that love with someone else. I would like to finish this book by giving you the opportunity to understand how this is possible and then give you an opportunity to receive this amazing love.

*****

Thousands of years ago, God established rules with mankind that they had to follow, for them to be in right standing (or considered righteous) with God. This was known as the *Torah*, and it consisted of six hundred and eleven rules that was known as *the Law*. If someone broke any of these laws, which everyone did because of how many there were, they would have to sacrifice animals to atone for their sins. This was consistent across all of God's people, and it is also consistent with how God covered Adam and Eve after they sinned in the garden of Eden.

> But now God has shown us a way to be made right with him without keeping the requirements of the

law, as was promised in the writings of Moses and the prophets long ago. We are made right with God by placing our faith in Jesus Christ. And this is true for everyone who believes, no matter who we are. For everyone has sinned; we all fall short of God's glorious standard. Yet God, in his grace, freely makes us right in his sight. He did this through Christ Jesus when he freed us from the penalty for our sins. For God presented Jesus as the sacrifice for sin. People are made right with God when they believe that Jesus sacrificed his life, shedding his blood. (Romans 3:21–25a, NLT)

This explains why Jesus came to earth. The reason he came to the earth to die was so by His sacrifice, we could all be made righteous through is death. Instead of us continuing to atone for our sins, by killing animals, God sent His own Son to earth to be a living sacrifice for us. If we are willing to place our faith in God to forgive our sins, believe that Jesus was the Son of God, and He truly did die so we could have eternal life, we are made righteous through believing that.

Verse 23 explains that we have all sinned and fallen short of God's standards to go to heaven. It's important that we understand that God is holy, meaning He is set apart and cannot be in relationship with sin. God and sin are like oil and water; they don't mix. Therefore, every human being who has ever done something wrong is guilty of sin and isn't qualified to be righteous. The worst person on earth and the most moral person are both in need of the same grace of God. This is why Jesus Christ's sacrifice was necessary—to pay the price that we deserved to pay. If we are willing to accept that grace (or free gift that we don't deserve), we are free from needing to uphold all six hundred and eleven laws to be considered righteous in God's eyes. When God looks at us, He sees His Son's sacrifice, not our sin.

Well then, since God's grace has set us free from the law, does that mean we can go on sinning?

Of course not! Don't you realize that you become the slave of whatever you choose to obey? You can be a slave to sin, which leads to death, or you can choose to obey God, which leads to righteous living. Thank God! Once you were slaves of sin, but now you wholeheartedly obey this teaching we have given you. Now you are free from your slavery to sin, and you have become slaves to righteous living.

Because of the weakness of your human nature, I am using the illustration of slavery to help you understand all this. Previously, you let yourselves be slaves to impurity and lawlessness, which led ever deeper into sin. Now you must give yourselves to be slaves to righteous living so that you will become holy.

When you were slaves to sin, you were free from the obligation to do right. And what was the result? You are now ashamed of the things you used to do, things that end in eternal doom. But now you are free from the power of sin and have become slaves of God. Now you do those things that lead to holiness and result in eternal life. For the wages of sin is death, but the free gift of God is eternal life through Christ Jesus our Lord. (Romans 6:15–23, NLT)

The Bible uses this term "slave" because the people of that time would have made a strong connection with what being a slave entailed. This text explains that before accepting God's free gift of righteousness, we are actually slaves to our bad intentions. Inside each and every one of us, we have something called passions of the flesh (1 Peter 2:11) that the Bible says "wage war" against our soul, meaning those times when you really don't want to do something and you know the consequences are going to be bad, but you still have a craving to do it so badly that you give in and do it anyway—this is what the Bible means when it says that you are a slave to those evil desires. Regardless of how hard you fight to suppress them, eventually you will succumb to the temptation and give in. What God does when you receive his gift of righteousness is He puts the same Holy Spirit that was in Jesus Christ (Mark 1:9–11) inside of you, and the Holy Spirit gives you the ability to resist those passions and choose not to give in. Notice the Bible doesn't tell us that we won't *want* to do those bad things anymore, it says that we will have the right to no longer be slaves. The choice now becomes ours to choose to follow the evil desires or follow the voice of the Holy Spirit within us. If you've seen the cartoon of the angel on one shoulder and the devil on the other, this is a great representation of what happens when we become Christians. Our flesh and our spirit fight each other for the battlefield of our mind.

> For Moses writes that the law's way of making a person right with God requires obedience to all of its commands. But faith's way of getting right with God says, "Don't say in your heart, 'Who will go up to heaven?' (to bring Christ down to earth). And don't say, 'Who will go down to the place of the dead?' (to bring Christ back to life again)." In fact, it says, "The message is very close at hand; it is on your lips and in your heart."
>
> And that message is the very message about faith that we preach: If you openly declare that Jesus is Lord and believe in your heart that God raised him from the dead, you will be saved. For it is by believing in your heart that you are made right with God, and it is by openly declaring your faith that you are saved. As the Scriptures tell us, "Anyone who trusts in him will never be disgraced." Jew and Gentile are the same in this respect. They have the same Lord, who gives generously to all who call on him. For "Everyone

who calls on the name of the Lord will be saved."
(Romans 10:5–13, NLT)

This is salvation. I want to apologize for any church, pastor, self-proclaimed Christian, or organization that has ever told you that becoming a child of God requires anything more or less than this. God's Word is extremely clear that for you to be saved from an eternity in hell and spend eternity after you die in heaven, all you must do is as follows:

- Believe that Jesus Christ was who He said He was—The Son of God in a human body, who was born of a virgin, impregnated by the power of the Holy Spirit (Matthew 1:18, Luke 1:26–35, Isaiah 7:14).
- He did what the Bible says He did—Came to the earth, lived a sinless life, died on the cross, and was raised to life three days later, ultimately defeating death so we could be made righteous through Him paying the punishment that we rightfully deserved (John 3:16–17).
- Accept His free gift of salvation through faith—Believe that through His sacrifice on the cross, you don't have to do *anything* to earn your salvation, but believe that it is a free gift for all those who choose to accept and believe it (Ephesians 2:8–9).
- Confess with your mouth—Declare out loud that you know you are a sinner and you need a Savior; that you believe Christ died specifically for you and, by confessing it out loud, that God hears you and saves you from an eternity separated from Him; and that you know there's nothing you can do to add to or take away from Christ's sacrifice, but only need to accept and believe it.

*****

This is the single most important decision that you will make in your life. If you have already made this decision, I thank God that you have, and I pray that the Holy Spirit would continue to stir up the passion to love your players in a way that you never have. Remember that there is no limit to the growth that you can discover in your walk with Christ. The Holy Spirit wants to take over in every area of your life. He doesn't just want access to the parts that you have cleaned up; He wants to come into every room of your house and transform it to look like Christ. Please keep in mind that God is a perfect gentleman. He's not going to force you to do anything that you don't want to do. You must allow Him to have access to the places in your life that don't reflect Him. He is patient and will wait for you to surrender those things over to Him. I thank God for our relationship as brothers and sisters in Christ, and I pray that as fellow coaches, we will shake the foundations of hell as we bring God's kingdom into our programs with how we love our players!

If you have not made this decision, I pray that today will be the day that you decide to change your life for eternity. Revelation 3:20 says, "Behold, I stand at the door and knock. If anyone hears My voice and opens the door, I will come in to him and dine with him, and he with Me."

Some of you, as you have been going through this book, God has been knocking on the door of your heart. You've felt Him drawing you toward Him, and maybe for the first time, you're hearing His voice. It might be scary, but there's something about it that brings you hope and security. There may be dozens of questions that you don't have answers to, but you still find yourself wanting to reach out to Him. I'm asking you right now to take that step, open your mouth, and talk to God.

There is no better time than right now to make that commitment to follow Jesus Christ. You don't need to clean yourself up. You don't need to kick that awful habit you can't seem to break, and you don't need to wait until you have all the answers. I have been a Christian for twenty years, and there are still things that I can't fully explain. That is why God requires us to have faith. There are going to be questions that you have the rest of your life, and you might not get them all answered, but God asks us to put our faith in Him. The truth is we all put our faith in something. Are you willing to put your faith in Jesus? Are you willing to let God, who designed every aspect of your being, into your life so that He can love you in ways you've never experienced?

If you want to make that choice, we are going to do that right now. I want you to say this prayer out loud.

> God, I thank You that You loved me enough to send Your one and only Son to die on the cross so that I could spend eternity with You. I know that I am a sinner, and I don't deserve the incredible gift of salvation that the Bible says You offer me. You Word says if I believe in my heart that Jesus died for my sins and I confess with my mouth that You have permission to be Lord of my life, You will come into my heart and save me. I thank You that you hear me and that You created me with a purpose to glorify You with my life. I give You permission to change me from the inside out, and I will spend the rest of my life trying to serve You and live the way Your Word instructs me to live. Amen.

If you said that prayer, I am overjoyed to celebrate with you and tell you that you are a Christian! The spirit of God now lives on the inside of you, and your name is written on the palm of God's hand. The Bible actually says that God gets a tattoo of your name on Himself (Isaiah 49:16)!

There are some things that you need to be prepared for moving forward. Being a Christ-follower means you have just become number one on Satan's wanted list. Our enemy is terrified of Christ-followers, because of the power that is inside of them. This is not a life for the faint at heart. Living a life glorifying to God promises to come with adversity. Jesus Himself was never tempted for twenty-nine years, and then after being baptized by John the Baptist, Satan showed up to tempt him. The devil isn't concerned with you, until you discover your identity from your heavenly Father.

You need to be on guard for attacks, as you are starting your relationship as a new believer. Thoughts of doubt, insecurity—"Did one simple prayer really change my life?"—and many others could begin to rise up in you. That is why you need to start studying the Word. Romans 12:2 says, "Do not conform to the patterns of this world, but be transformed by the renewing of your mind." This leads me to my second piece of instruction.

You are a three-part being. You are a spirit, you have a soul, and you live in a body. The reason for this is because you were made in the image and likeness of God (Genesis 1:26–28). Your spirit has just been made alive in Christ Jesus, but the Bible says that your mind and your body weren't affected by your spiritual transformation. This is why you might not *feel* a lot different over the next few days or weeks. Our responsibility now is to grow in our knowledge and understanding of God's Word, and what will start to happen is you will begin having new desires. The things you used to do won't seem fun or satisfying anymore. The way you used to talk will make you feel different when the words come out of your mouth. God is going to take you through a process called sanctification, where you will slowly begin to look more like Him, as you grow in your relationship. Sanctification can sound like a really intimidating word, but what it means is just like when a married couple begins to look like each other time, the same thing will begin to happen to you. The reason spouses begin to look alike is because they spend so much time together and are so intimate that their outward appearance begins to reflect their intimacy. The same will begin to happen with you and God as you walk through life with Him. Don't be discouraged if you find yourself struggling at first with the same temptations you had before you committed to following Jesus. Sanctification is a marathon, not a sprint.

My third and final piece of advice is to surround yourself with other believers who will help you grow and keep you accountable. The people that we surround ourselves with directly affect our thoughts, attitudes, and decisions. You would be wise to find a local church that you can join so you can begin to build life-giving relationships. Get involved and find ways to serve. Join a small group so you can study God's Word with other believers and do life with other people who desire to see you grow. As we talked about before, God designed us to be in community, and we need to be intentional about who is in our inner circle.

The life of a Christian can be filled with joy, excitement, hope, and most of all *agape* when you seek to grow daily. As you strive to learn more about your Creator, you are going to also learn about who you are. You are going to discover things about yourself that you never knew were inside of you, because they have always been hidden in your spirit that has been made alive. I would love to answer any questions or comments that you may have, and if you made the decision to accept Jesus as your Lord and Savior, it would bless me tremendously to know you made that commitment. My e-mail address is coachmcbeth12@gmail.com

The life of a *Sweet Sixteen* coach starts and ends with being rooted and ground in your faith. A coach can only reflect what has already taken place within them. We love, because He first loved us. I pray that you will let God be the foundation of your coaching philosophy and that you would pray daily, study the Bible, be quick to ask for forgiveness, and surround yourself with godly people. May you find success in every season of your life, and may you always give God the glory.

> For I am convinced that neither death nor life, neither angels nor demons, neither the present nor the future, nor any powers, neither height nor depth, nor anything else in all creation, will be able to separate us from the love of God that is in Christ Jesus our Lord. (Romans 8:38–39, NIV)

May God show you favor and success as you go on your journey to *The Sweet Sixteen*.

About the Author

Austin McBeth is from Wayland, Iowa. He spent the majority of his life being involved in sports. After finishing high school, Austin attended North Iowa Area Community College (NIACC) in Mason City, Iowa, to play both basketball and football. He then transferred to Iowa Western Community College in Council Bluffs, Iowa, to become the first quarterback in the program's history. Austin accepted an offer to play football at Iowa State University after his redshirt freshman season. After a year playing quarterback, he walked on to the basketball team to play for newly appointed head coach Fred Hoiberg.

McBeth felt he was called by God to become a collegiate basketball coach as he entered his senior season and spent his last year as a Cyclone preparing for life after basketball. He has coached at the NAIA, junior college, and now Division 2 level as he enters his seventh coaching season. His passion is to teach the game of basketball while living a life that glorifies God and points his players to the hope he has found in Jesus Christ.

His dream is to one day be a head coach and continue using his daily influence to be a big brother and father figure to his players with the help and incredible support of his wife Jennifer.

CPSIA information can be obtained
at www.ICGtesting.com
Printed in the USA
LVHW020035310520
656910LV00006B/429